REVIEWS

"The messages and beautiful stories in this book will not only uplift your mind but touch your heart and soul. Now more than ever we need to understand, believe in and stand for love. The power of love will change and heal the world - grab this book as your guide." ~ Shannon Kaiser, bestselling author of *The Self-Love Experiment* and *Joy Seeker* | @shannonkaiserwrites

"*Dear Love* is exactly the book so many women need right now – exactly the book I needed right now. A compelling reminder – from women who've struggled with self-love their whole lives – that self-doubt and imposter syndrome cripples us, stalls us, keeps us from reaching our potential, and from loving, accepting and celebrating ourselves. Their stories will motivate and uplift you. They'll make you feel like you have a sisterhood of women cheering you on, encouraging you to look deep inside and let go of years of guilt and a critical self-talk. To look in the mirror and finally love who you see. A must-read for all women, young and old." ~ Kristen Thompson, Editor, Journalist, and Publisher of DoTheOkanagan.com

"'Learn your truth... share your authentic self.' Habiba Jessica Zaman (author of chapter 10) is raw and real. She speaks of finding love within yourself and owning your truth. You don't have to be married or single to know when you are ready for love. You have to start to fall in love first with yourself again and remember what fuels your passion for life. Zaman is an inspiration." - M. Bergin, Ohio Working Soccer Mom Tribe

DEAR LOVE

I'M READY FOR YOU

DEAR LOVE

I'M READY FOR YOU

by Sara Gustafson

contributing authors: Christine Esovoloff, Pam Davis, Apryl Norkett, Carley Inglis, Roberta Fernandez, Chelsea Forrest, Heather Lee Chapman, Jess Harvey, Saira Amjad, Habiba Jessica Zaman, J.R. Huff, Danielle Laura, Corinne Walsh Stratton, Jess Reidell, Maryann Perri, Tamara Simpers, Mandy Valpey

GOLDEN BRICK ROAD
PUBLISHING HOUSE

CONTENTS

foreword

BY: KY-LEE HANSON

PUBLISHER AND CREATOR OF THE *DEAR WOMEN* SERIES

Dear Love, I'm Ready for You was an addition I needed in my life and to the *Dear Women* book series. I feel books find you when you need them, and in my case as a publisher, authors find me when they need my help to share their story. Little they may know I need to hear their story, too. We started this series with *Dear Stress, I'm Breaking Up with You,* which discussed internal, external, career, family, and health stressors women commonly face, with a goal to provide clarity on situations. With a clearer mind and stress management practices, we can then look at the limitations blocking us such as our relationship with money, our relationships in general, or our self-limiting beliefs - we explored these topics in the award-winning *Dear Limits, Get Out of My Way.* After these two books, we had a clearer sense of purpose and wondered how to best use it. *Dear Time, Are You on My Side?* is a two-time award-winning, thought-provoking book that has become a favorite to many. Now, *Dear Love, I'm Ready for You* is a book I could not genuinely write. It was the book that wanted to be the fourth progression of the series, but as for the thought of *me* as the lead contributing author . . . I did not have the confidence in myself to write about the topic of self-love. It was a journey I needed to go on, the next brick to lay on my golden path, but one I was avoiding at all costs.

Divinely, I found friendship and partnership in Sara Gustafson and she took such great care of putting together this book. I may have thought this was to be an "easier" journey than ones I had been on before. *Learning to love the self — what is that? Spa visits, reading, journaling, affirmations — sure, I can do that!* Wow was I ever wrong. I am sure a large part of me knew there was more to it, which was the reason for my aversion. I knew it would be disruptive; things in all aspects of my life were deeply due for a change. Self-love arrived this past year and *blew up* much of what I thought to be a solid foundation.

Looking back, how did I allow myself to be within such an external, demanding, environment for so long? I am a strong, confident, intelligent, nurturing woman — how was I so blind to what was happening *to me*? My desire to help others had left me in a state of over-giving: drained, burned out, and financially support-ing countless people. I am a self-made entrepreneur, so this responsibility I had allowed onto myself had become a great force. Everyone and everything else came first, always — clients, contractors, family, friends, projects, charities — and I was forgiving and accommodating of every request, want, and need asked of me. *What more can I do? Is this how I will feel included and supported?* I looked out for myself by making sure those around me were comfortable. Seeing people struggle was my greatest discomfort, so I would tell myself I could personally take on more of the world's weight.

As this book came into fruition and I became more aware of self-love and how greatly I lacked it, my interest turned to setting boundaries and becoming more approachable. Those together don't make a whole of a lot of sense but learning something new rarely does. What I was ultimately looking for was a new circle of people. I wanted boundaries from the friends and supporters that only seemed to communicate with me when it was work, money, or favor-related, and I wanted people to reach out to me who were willing to understand me, who wanted to be a genuine friend. I felt alone while being surrounded by people.

Months into the year of feeling this way, some new people showed up in my life, and other relationships became deeper, through observing their openness with mental health, adult bullying, the hard lessons of love from any type of relationship, I decided therapy was the next brick to lay on my personal path. Through this act of self-love, healthy boundaries started to form, and I started to put out the acces-sibility I wanted to put out. I took time to listen to myself and understand what is energetically beneficial and what I have to say "no" to. I was looking for qualities in people I could admire and learn from, and who were also curious about me; I wanted all of my relationships to be like a two-way street. True partnerships and collaborations to create a better world are the things that light me up!

As the boundaries began to go up and I was coming to terms with the fact that I had allowed myself to become a "people pleaser", people resisted the change, and I went through months of people digging up the bricks I laid behind me and using them as weapons to cripple me. It didn't work. You see, since I had found self-love, it was now my invisible armor. I was changing my life's narrative. I told myself I would no longer allow people to bully or use me. As hard as this time in my life was, I had a real support group around me but to be honest . . . it took time and healing for me to realize I deserved them. Having people around me that wanted nothing from me except just to see me be okay, I *could* be okay. I could be okay with everything that happened to me and start to rebuild in a new environment. My new circle of people could see me for me, and they began to help me see myself too. Some of those people are the authors of this book. This project has been the most beautiful I have been a part of to date. A book title tends to embody the conception and development of itself. Love comes in many shapes and forms, and through many people, to teach us something new. The stories in this book helped me get through one of the two hardest things I have been though in my thirty-four years here on earth. I couldn't be more grateful.

Sometimes I mundanely think we might be here to learn suffering, but maybe we are here to learn that love in all its forms triumphs all.

Introduction

BY: SARA GUSTAFSON

GROWING UP, WE'RE TAUGHT THAT four-letter words hold a lot of weight. They're dangerous, powerful, the ones that make people stop and take note.

I think it's no coincidence that love, too, is a four-letter word. Love can expose us to the most painful kinds of hurt, loss, and betrayal. Love can also crack us open, widen our worlds, and heal our souls like no other force on earth. The brave souls in this book have let love do just that.

The kind of love described in these pages is *real*. You won't find any Disney stories here, no fluffy, sanitized fairy tales. The wise women who joined this beautiful project did so for precisely that reason. They wanted to share real-life love stories, to shatter the rosy veneer that so often accompanies the word "love." They knew that we do a disservice to our stories, our loves, and ultimately ourselves when we try to gloss over the nasty bits.

Love can transform us, but as the stories in this book show, that process is not always pretty. We all know that love is patient, love is kind. But love is also messy. It is complicated. It is difficult. Love is ferocious. It has teeth and like a mother wolf snarling at her pups, it is not afraid to bare them to teach us important lessons. Love is not for the weak of heart.

My friend Jeff, whom you'll read more about in my chapter, once told me, "Life isn't some tea party where everything is all set up and in place. That's not perfect; that's sickening. Life is a roller coaster, and it's perfect." We can say the same of love, I think. If we wait around for the "perfect" love to appear, we'll end up a very lonely bag of bones. But more importantly, even if we ultimately found that "perfect" fairy-tale love, it wouldn't do what we want it to do, what love is *meant* to do. And that is to change us, to make us better versions of ourselves. Love's challenges are exactly what make it perfect.

I believe deeply in the power of love to change and heal our world. To do that, it needs to be the kind of love described in these chapters. Strong, fierce, unapologetic love, the kind that does not back down from a fight. In today's world of Instagram spirituality, "love and light" are often used to bypass life's harsher realities. Real love, the kind my co-authors share so vulnerably, does not do that. Real love looks fear in the eye. It admits when it is wrong. It fights injustice and hate. It acts in righteous anger when it needs to so that we can all rise together. As Dr. Clarissa Pinkola Estés says in *Women Who Run with the Wolves*, "[l]ove is not neutral. It takes a stand. It is a commitment to the attainment of the conditions of peace for everyone."[1]

For love to transform us and our world, we must be open to receiving it. It sounds simple, but so often we reject love or even flat-out don't see it because it doesn't look the way we thought it would. Love doesn't just come in the form of romantic relationships. It comes into our lives in all sorts of guises, from romance to family relationships, from friendships to community to (my personal favorite) our relationship with ourselves. Not to sound too cheesy, but to quote one of my all-time favorite movies, "Love actually is *all around*."[2] If we're fixated on finding one specific relationship, one specific kind of love, who knows what treasures we will miss? As the stories in this book show, when we open ourselves up to receiving love in all of its forms, magical things can happen.

I hope these pages inspire you to love more deeply, to be more open to receiving love in your life no matter its form, to embrace the power of this four-letter word, and to let it work through you to heal us all.

SECTION 1

READY TO LOVE MYSELF

I AM INFINITELY LOVED
AND DIVINELY SUPPORTED,
PURPOSEFULLY WHOLE
WITHIN MY OWN HEART.

CHAPTER 1

A Non-Linear Kind of Love

"For me, self-love means sharing my feelings without worrying about being rejected. It means admitting when I mess up, because I am worthy of love regardless of my flaws."

BY: CHRISTINE ESOVOLOFF

Christine Esovoloff

https://christineesovoloff.home.blog

ig: @the_ginger_journal

. . . .

TENACIOUS, FIERY, ENTHUSIASTIC, and funny: these are the words Christine's friends used to describe her when she asked for a little feedback for this biography. That and indecisive, but she thought that would be best left out. So how does Christine describe herself? As a laughter lover, awkwardness expert, gratitude enthusiast, food and wine connoisseur, and self-love devotee!

An advertising sales executive by day and a rock star writer by night (assuming rock stars go to bed at nine), Christine has always had a passion for telling stories and entertaining people. She got her first writing gig on a whim when she offered to be a columnist for an online newspaper, and things just took off from there. When her career in sales required her to leave the column behind, she started a blog to keep up with her passion.

Christine resides in sunny Okanagan, BC, with her kids, fiancé, and dog. When she is not sipping Okanagan wine with loved ones, you can usually find her hiking or getting bendy in a hot yoga class.

WHEN I FIRST GOT THE OPPORTUNITY to write a chapter in this book, I was thrilled. I was excited, inspired, and if I'm being completely honest a little cocky. I have always been the girl with *lots* to say. And as for the subject of love, specifically self-love? Well, that's been something I've been working on for a while, so I figured I had this whole thing locked down. I planned on sharing the story of my childhood, of how I used to chase the love and approval of others but now had come to a place of loving the self. Sure, I am still working on my shit, but for the most part, I am comfortable in my own skin and happy with who I see in the mirror. This chapter was going to be the perfect blend of vulnerability and humor. It was going to further my healing and hopefully provide a little inspiration to others.

It was going to be easy. How could it not be?! After all, I had come so far.

I was in for a pretty rude and humbling awakening.

Surprisingly, as the girl who always has something to say, I found myself drawing a blank. I found myself frustrated and in tears, full of angst and doubt.

Who did I think I was? I can't inspire anyone. My childhood wasn't even that bad. Who was I kidding? I haven't healed. I can't write. I'm not nearly as talented as the other women in this book. I bet I'm not as pretty. Not as smart. Not as authentic. Not as wounded. Not as evolved. Not as accomplished. A fraud.

I found myself angry, sensitive, and anxious.

I sent draft after draft to friends asking for their feedback, only to get defensive at their constructive criticism or question the truthfulness of their praise. I was snappy with my children. I was, out of nowhere, a depressed, insecure little girl again. What the hell was happening?

How did I go from thinking *I've come so far! I am worthy of this opportunity!* to feeling like a farce and questioning everything about myself?

It turns out I didn't have self-love as locked down as I thought. It turns out I still very much look to others for approval. It turns out this whole healing and self-love thing is not linear at all. I don't know why this came as a bit of a surprise to me. I mean, I have read enough self-help books and spent enough time in counselors' offices to know that this process can be a "one step forward, two steps back" kind of thing, but it was startling to see how much my opinion of myself still depends on how others see me. If my friends think I am smart/funny/successful, then I am smart/funny/successful. If men think I am beautiful, then I am beautiful. If the world tells me I am worthy of love, then I have permission to love myself.

So where does all this crap come from? Why are we all big balls of insecurity? I think in a lot of cases, it starts during childhood. At least, that's where it started for me.

I think we all receive messages at some point that we are not good enough or not lovable. We see images of what we should look like on billboards, in magazines, and on TV. We get criticized by our peers and our parents, we get rejected, we get told we aren't smart enough. We endure trauma and hurt. It is endless, and I am amazed any of us even leave our house.

When I sat down and really examined what messages I was still grappling with and how I had come to this place of self-doubt and loathing, I found myself both surprised and saddened by how much crap I still carry with me and by how I was still making so many of those lies into my truth, despite all the work I had done.

The messages started when I was very young. I was an only child raised by a single mother. I had been the product of an affair, so my fifty-something father had no interest in me. My mother struggled with mental illness, self-harm, and alcoholism. She was often very dissociative and unavailable as a result of her illness, and that left me feeling alone and very hungry for love and acceptance.

I remember her telling me how "intense" I was as a young child, how she used to worry because I would hop on the lap of any stranger, engage almost anyone in conversation. I learned very early on that if I wanted attention I would have to go out and get it. And I did. My mission in life became to gain the approval and love of others to find where I belonged.

My search for belonging led me in many directions throughout my youth, many of them self-destructive, which just furthered the shame and self-loathing I was trying to escape.

I have come a long way since that awkward little girl with frizzy red hair who scraped by in school and sucked at sports, but I still very much strive to please people. In fact, much of what I do is an attempt to prove to others and myself that I am funny, smart, pretty, or successful. When it came to writing this chapter, I realized that I didn't sign up for this journey because I think I am a talented writer worthy of this opportunity. I signed up for this so other people would tell me that I am.

Needless to say, when I had this realization, I had a mini-breakdown.

What does one do when they come to the crushing realization that they really do not love themselves as much as they thought they did? That rather, they are a big ball of insecurity and self-judgement? What does one do when they realize that loving the self is not a straightforward process with a finish line? That there are no winners or losers?

Well, I did what I normally do when things go awry: I wallowed in misery for a while.

In a world in which we are always inundated with messages such as #positivity, #yougotthis, and #happiness, I think it is quite therapeutic to pout, eat too much cheesecake, and feel sorry for yourself for a bit, but only for a bit. Because the truth is that sometimes we don't feel positive. Sometimes we most certainly do not feel like "we've got this." Sometimes we are lost and scared, and denying that by hiding behind a cheery internet-worthy front is not helpful.

Sometimes getting real with our feelings by soaking in them for a bit is a great place to start getting past them.

Trying to avoid yucky feelings is kind of like trying to sneak past border patrol. First of all, good luck. They are ruthless MOFOs. And second of all, if you do manage to get past them, it doesn't matter how fast you run or how well you hide, those buggers are going to find you and it is going to hurt so much more than if you had just dealt with them head-on in the first place. Think ass-kicking and cavity searches. It is just as true with feelings as it is with cranky border cops: both will rough you up if you try to escape or avoid them.

The truth is, I needed to take some time to examine things. I needed to go through the process of looking at my childhood and identifying what messages I had received, if or why I was still buying into them, and how I was going to attempt to work through them. Most importantly I needed to figure out what the hell self-love even meant.

It is difficult to pursue a goal if you aren't even clear on what it is you are after.

When I sat down and really thought about what it means to love myself, I found it difficult to pin down. In fact, I couldn't really tell you what self-love meant. All I really knew was that I wanted more of it. No wonder I was struggling! In order to achieve a goal, you have to be able to define it. The more specific and defined your goal, the more likely you are to attain it. For example, if my goal is to be healthier, I am probably going to have a hard time achieving that goal because it is way too broad. But if I can break it down and define what being healthy means to me, I can start whacking away at it in small chunks. And being healthy to me may mean something very different than being healthy to someone else. Hence the need to define our own personal goals and get specific.

So how do you define something like "self-love" when you have no idea where to start? My trick is to work backwards.

Let's use the example of health. If you close your eyes and picture yourself at a fantastic level of health, what do you see? For me, I see someone who has energy, who is active every day, and who gets lots of sleep. I see someone who fills her body with healthy food and lots of fresh water. I see strength, and I see lots of yoga.

Now I have something to work with. I can start setting small, achievable goals that fit within my definition of "great health." I can join a yoga studio, commit to eight hours of sleep a night, and incorporate veggies into at least two meals a day.

The same goes for self-love. Spend some time picturing yourself at a ten out of ten in the self-love department. What do you see? It will vary for everyone. You may see someone who stands up for themselves, who leaves behind crappy relationships, who reaches out for help, or who asks for that damn promotion because they know they deserve it.

For me, self-love means sharing my feelings without worrying about being rejected. It means admitting when I fuck up, because I am worthy of love regardless of my flaws. It means chasing success instead of sabotaging myself, because I am just as deserving and capable of success as anyone else. But mostly, it means finding a balance between forgiving myself when I falter (because this journey is not linear) and not giving up when it gets tough. It means being compassionate with myself while holding myself accountable for my actions and decisions.

Take some time to determine what messages you are stuck on, where they came from, and most importantly, what self-love means to you. Once we can get specific about what we are after, we become more aware of the areas that need a little work or the steps we need to take.

Oh yeah, and for the love of all that is good in the world, be gentle. Be gentle not only with yourself but with the people in your story. Which brings me to the last powerful nugget I discovered through this process.

Remember the importance of forgiveness. One of my favorite quotes is by author Kemi Sogunle: "*You cannot love if you cannot forgive.*" Man, is that the truth. A difficult truth but perhaps the most important one. At least, it was for me.

When you start digging around to figure out how you got to this place of self-doubt, stuff is going to come up. Whether it is anger, sadness, pain, or resentment, and whether these emotions are self-directed or focused at others, they are the biggest roadblocks when it comes to self-love. After all, it is pretty hard to love and accept yourself when you are a stewing pit of anger and shame.

How do we forgive? For me, the answer was understanding and empathy. Looking back on my past, I saw a lot of people who hurt or abandoned me, whether intentionally or not. And when I was able to understand that these people had also endured pain, rejection, trauma, or abandonment, and in a lot of cases they were just not able to do better, it became easier to forgive them. In extreme cases, I just had to picture them as tiny babies — whatever works. The bottom line is that forgiveness is more about freeing ourselves than freeing the other person.

The same principle applies when it comes to self-forgiveness. I have messed up. I have missed opportunities. I have hurt people. And I have carried a bunch of misplaced shame along with me for too long. But when I can have some understanding and cut myself some damn slack, I free myself up to be able to make some real change.

Part of the change for me was learning that it is okay to look to others for approval and love. I think it is very natural, primal, and hard-wired within us to desire acceptance from our family and peers. Seeking love and acceptance from others doesn't mean that I cannot or do not love myself, too. The two are not mutually exclusive.

Perhaps signing up to write this chapter was the biggest act of self-love of all. Sure, I want others to encourage me and approve of my work — that is natural. But on some level, I signed up because I believed in myself. I invested in my dream. I didn't back down when it got hard or scary. And I gave myself permission to be vulnerable.

That is *love*. At least, that is my definition of it.

The reality is that this journey of self-love is never done. It's messy and it's hard and sometimes, we might have to face things about ourselves that we don't really like. But when we can shelve the judgement, figure out what self-love really means to us, and offer ourselves a bit of compassion along the way, we can make the process just a little easier. By being gentle and loving with ourselves, we can free up space to start seeing and falling in love with all our potential. And while falling in love with someone's potential can be dangerous and frustrating, when it comes to our relationship with ourselves, it is wonderful. When we see our own potential, we realize we have the power and capacity to take a brave step. To go after our dreams. To change our lives.

I DO NOT HAVE TO BE PERFECT TO BE LOVED.

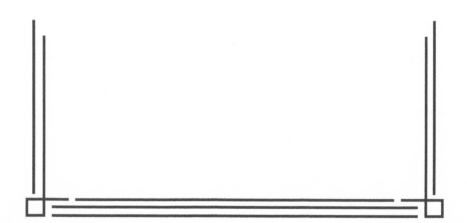

CHAPTER 2

How I Learned to Be My Own Best Love Teacher

"Say yes to yourself, maybe for the first time, and see what happens."

BY: PAM DAVIS

Pam Davis

coachpamdavis.com | coachpamdavis@gmail.com

ig: @coachpamdavis | fb: @coachpamdavis

. . . .

PAM DAVIS IS A coach, teacher, writer, and late bloomer who guides women and men who are ready to increase the love, joy, and meaning in their lives. Her late-in-life journey to self-love was the beginning of every part of her life changing. Now she shares her story and her strengths with others as they learn to love themselves, right where they are now.

Pam became a Catalyst Life Coach with JRNI and now works for that company as the Class Coach for all incoming students. She also has her own coaching practice and focuses on self-love and supporting others along their road to self-compassion and acceptance. She loves to laugh, hug, and get to know you. Gratitude, creativity, and community matter. She hears your heart before you do.

Pam's proudest milestones are leaving her job of thirty years to create her new path and finding a bridge to peace and love with her mom before she died. It's never too late to start the next chapter!

Standing on the campus in my cap and gown, I could barely believe I was about to graduate from college. It had been a long road. I was forty-seven years old, and finishing my degree had not been a straight line. There was a time, decades ago, when I thought it was impossible, when I believed I was incapable of passing the required math and science classes. I would attempt my most difficult classes, but after a few weeks I would stop attending and receive a failing grade. I convinced myself that I was stupid and unable to pass those two classes. Shame, self-hate, and negative thoughts ran my life. Eventually they asked me to leave college — I was kicked out for my low GPA. Now, being on campus waiting for them to call me to the graduation stage, a new perception of myself was about to be born.

For as long as I could remember, I have felt *less than*. I convinced myself that I was not enough as I was and that I was stupid and unlovable. I felt unworthy of love and attention. While my family loved me, I did not feel loved. I felt invisible. I do not remember many days after the age of six when I felt okay. Later in life, the failed math and science classes were just further proof of my deficiencies. The lowly job I accepted was all I thought I could expect.

Somewhere along the way in these early years, I decided to need less and not to take up too much space or make too much noise. In a way, it's hard to complain — I had two parents, a home, food, clothes, and some extras. I was cared for in the best way they knew how. But to a young alcoholic mother, I was also often an inconvenience. Being quiet and small was my way of gaining acceptance and praise: "She is such a good little girl, no bother at all. She is so self-sufficient and only seven years old." My little heart would swell with each breadcrumb of praise, so I did more "good girl" things. And in those acts, I felt less unlovable, if only for a moment. I acted out these early beliefs and carried around these thoughts for decades.

When I went back to school in my forties, I thought I was attempting once again to fulfill my dream of becoming a teacher. Little did I know that I would find the real me by disproving two of the lies I had been telling myself: I was stupid, and I was not good enough to be a teacher. I learned so many lessons outside the classroom that started my unexpected self-love expedition. This time I realized I did not have to do it alone, so I got a math and science tutor. In the past, I had not thought to ask for help because I had not felt worthy of support. But by getting the help I needed, I earned As in those classes I had failed multiple times. In doing so, I proved to myself that I was not stupid.

The courageous act of starting again, along with some help and a new perspective, would end up changing the course of my life. I am glad I received my degree, but I am even more grateful that I permitted myself to find my unique definition of self-love and acceptance.

I heard my name called and walked across the stage to receive my diploma. On my graduation sash, I had attached pictures of all the people who had supported and loved me as I finally completed all my classes. Many loved me, though I did not let myself feel their love. Fifteen people showed up to celebrate my graduation. I imagined they were just being kind and they felt sorry for me — another story I told myself to continue my path of self-hatred. As I walked toward this circle of friends, I saw a sudden wash of love and big smiles of genuine pride on all their faces. I turned to look behind me to see who they were smiling at, and in one instant, I realized — they were lighting up for *me*. All these lovely humans were proud of me. They loved me. They supported me. They wanted the best for me. No strings attached. It was like a huge love cloud that enveloped my whole being, and I could not ignore it.

In this moment, I had a powerful true knowing. These people loved me, and they were not lying. In their eyes, I was wholly, truly lovable. They didn't just love me for the strong parts or for what I could give them. They didn't see just sections of me. Rather, they saw the dark, the light, and all the shades and hues in between. In fact, they loved me for my vulnerable side as much as, and probably more than, for the highly responsible woman I strived to be.

A question started to form. What if I could see myself the way they all saw me? I did not know at the time, but this was the beginning of a whole new kind of education.

"May I learn to look at myself with the eyes of understanding and love."
~ Thích Nhất Hạnh

This question was my invitation to begin to see myself in a new way, and to disrupt some old ingrained beliefs. I would come to know these were false beliefs that could be dissolved, slowly, in bits, just like yours can. These were radical ideas, and every revolution has big consequences and costs. I was starting to be ready: ready to find out my worth and to commit to my healing, no matter how long it would take or what the costs would be.

A small quiet voice within was being heard. I could barely hear it but somehow, I knew it was there. When I thought of what I needed to look at first, I knew the way I spoke to myself had to change. I had a fierce, relentless inner critic, and that was the voice I heard loudest. Perhaps if I could turn down the volume on the inner critic, I might be able to hear that small voice of love deep within.

I gave myself a bottom line: *Don't do your own bad PR to yourself or others.*

This did not sound like me. Instead, this was the part of myself that wanted the best for me. I trusted, and I followed. The small voice was making sense, and it was getting stronger. I knew that if I changed the way I spoke to myself and about myself to others, it would lighten a big part of my struggle.

The process was slow and imperfect. I didn't do it perfectly. It took months and months to notice my inner monologue. I had decades of negative and critical self-talk to dismantle. Sometimes I could stop the talk in the moment. At other times, I still sounded pretty hateful, but the mess is mandatory. I just let myself practice this new way of being and talking to myself and within a few months, my life felt a little better. At about nine months, others started to notice I was no longer the butt of all my own jokes. Improving my self-talk made a big impact and affected all parts of my life.

In my self-love world, being harsh and critical was my biggest mountain to overcome; working with my inner critic helped me find more paths through which to build a clear, whole view of myself. I used to think when I loved myself, I would not speak so terribly to myself. It was just the opposite. In fact, when I stopped speaking so terribly to myself, I began to find real self-love and acceptance. For most clients with whom I work now, self-talk also makes a good first on-ramp on which to start to craft their self-love path.

What is *your* bottom line for how you will and will not speak to yourself?

> *"I now see how owning our story and loving ourselves through that process is the bravest thing that we will ever do."*
> ~ Brené Brown

This was my start on the road to self-love and a new way of seeing myself. I did not know all the how's, but I knew I wanted to keep going, to create this new world: one in which I believed in and accepted all parts of myself. With each step, I built the path. I could only see a foot or so ahead, but it was enough.

I needed more self-created guidelines as I started to uncover what it meant to be someone who loved herself. Gentleness, Patience, and Practice became my road buddies. They came one at a time.

Gentleness

One thing people always compliment me on is my calm, gentle nature. They don't hear my inner talk or my frustration on a packed freeway. My approach to others is to meet them with gentleness and acceptance. Being as kind to myself as I am with those I dearly love, or with anyone I meet on the street, did not come easily for me. I found it hard to accept myself as I am in this moment with gentleness and love. But we may give that gentleness to ourselves. Because I had always come from hardness, being gentle was exactly what I needed.

Patience

Another thing I often hear is, "Pam, you have so much patience." I worked with teens for many years and I love people in the most awkward and growth-filled years of life. I remember my own teen years: I wanted to fit in and I tried to do my best, but my hormones and life circumstances kept turning me upside down and making me feel all over the place. Seeing others as human and not expecting perfection from them came easily. I had plenty of patience for others. Seeing myself as human and giving myself grace was a different story. Adding in patience for myself was uncomfortable at first. I had to learn how to give it freely to myself. Because I had expected perfection for so many years, patience was exactly what I needed to blossom.

Practice

The third part of what I needed was to see all the new and big things I was learning about self-love and acceptance through the mindset of thinking it's all practice. I always felt like I had to get things right on the first try. Like many people, I struggled with perfectionism. I didn't finish my degree the first time through because it had not gone perfectly in a straight line. I needed to change my mindset. What if noticing my inner critic is just for practice? I can do that. What if talking to myself in a less harsh voice is just for practice? I'll try it. Letting myself see all that I was building as practice took away a huge amount of pressure. No one was grading me. Adding in the concept of "all is practice" gave me a much bigger playground on which to build my new way of living and loving myself. Practice over perfection was exactly what I needed to explore all parts of myself.

Ask yourself, "What do I need as I traverse each part of myself that I want to rebuild?" These examples are just the three things that seemed to appear for me, things I freely gave to others and was great at giving. Use them if they call to you. Make them your own. Add in what you need. You will know they are right when they feel big and scary. What do you need to take on the road with you as you build your new way of seeing yourself with love and acceptance?

It's now been about thirteen years since the night of my college graduation. I still have my sash with the pictures of my beloved friends and family. They are still in my corner. They loved me until I could love myself. I saw my scared and exquisite self in the mirror they were holding up for me.

To my utter delight and astonishment, I am now a self-love coach, teacher (yes, I am now a teacher), and coach/mentor to new Life Coaches. I help others to help themselves on their unique path to self-love. I even quit my thirty-year day job in early 2019. In no way would I have foreseen any of this at the start of my awakening. I only had the hope that I would stop hating myself and that, if I were really lucky, I might one day come to like myself. Self-care, finding my strengths, using my voice, letting go of past resentments, finding forgiveness for my mom and myself — all that came later.

> *"And the time came when the risk to remain tight in a bud*
> *was more painful than the risk it took to blossom."*
> ~ Anaïs Nin

Self-love is a practice. It keeps going and it keeps growing. I still see the next step only about twelve inches at a time, but now I think, *Wow, I never imagined I would be here!* My inner critic still tries to rear its ugly voice, and I let it. It's so much quieter and less harsh than when I started. Now it's actually hard for me to say something super critical of myself to others or to myself. I'm not in denial of my flaws. Rather, I am accepting of my humanness, flaws, strengths, and the whole being I am. Today when I find myself feeling critical or *less than*, I place my hand on my chest and say, "I'm here, I'm here," and I'm home again.

I started with a miniscule amount of hope. I reached out for support and tried lots of things that felt like they would lead me to each new step. I fell down and got back up, many times. I started by asking myself the question, "How would my life be different if I loved myself? I mean full-on, no conditions love rather than hate for myself?" I had no idea how this would happen, but I knew that something in me had shifted. I began to see people who were on my side, who supported me and cheered me on. In very small steps, I began to see ways to love myself. You can, too. This is your journey to take. Find your support and trust your inner knowing. The things that worked were unique to me and might differ from the things that work for others. Perhaps starting with your inner critic and adding in gentleness, patience, and practice might be helpful for you, too. Give yourself the freedom to experiment with them in a way that speaks to you. Create what you need and try things out. I am rooting you on and I believe in you because I remember what it felt like to be me, one day before my graduation.

Summon the smallest amount of hope you can and begin your self-love and acceptance adventure. It will not look the way you think it will look, and that is a good thing. I came to understand that I am my own best self-love teacher, and so are you! Say yes to yourself, maybe for the first time, and see what happens.

LOVE YOURSELF IN
THE WAY YOU WOULD
WANT SOMEONE TO
LOVE YOU, AND SEE
WHAT UNFOLDS.

CHAPTER 3

Four Steps to Lighten Up Your Life

"There comes a time when you need to stop being a victim to your past and stand up for your future."

BY: APRYL NORKETT

Apryl Norkett

ig: @aprylnorkett | fb: @AprylNorkett

. . . .

APRYL GREW UP IN OTTAWA, CANADA. Although she graduated high school with honors, she chose not to continue her studies out of a fear of not knowing what her passion was. After high school, Apryl moved to Toronto to try to start over. While the years passed, the same problems seemed to repeat themselves, so she began to teach herself different ways of dealing with life. Apryl has now studied numerous books and audios, and she has attended multiple conferences that deal with mental mastery. Researching alternative methods to benefit the body has also become a huge part of her life. She has now found her passion for personal development and growth and continues to help other people grow along with her. Her experience with depression in her early years continues to push her forward, and her caring and genuine personality want nothing but the best for everybody. In the future, Apryl hopes to create a retreat that helps people control their minds and boost their bodies using a variety of techniques.

IMAGINE A HUGE, INVISIBLE BAG, two or even three times your size, that you carry around everywhere on your back. What's in this bag? A whole lot of sadness, depression, anger, and every other negative emotion you can think of. The majority of people walk around with these enormous bags their entire lives. Wouldn't it be a lot easier to move forward, or in any direction, really, if we overcome these huge piles of baggage? But how on earth do we conquer that mountain if we don't even realize it's there?

Most of us simply don't have any idea that we live our lives based on traumatic experiences from our past. Names, places, events, times, songs: all these things and more can trigger us and remind us of the things in our past that hurt us. Can you think of something — an event, a place — that usually you would love, but for some reason, this time you just don't? Personally, I've been spotted crying on Christmas, which is supposed to be the happiest time of year, according to almost every Christmas carol ever made. I don't mean a little tear here and there, I'm talking about a full huffing, puffing, and wanting to launch the tree onto the snow kind of cry. I honestly love Christmas, and the fact that I was ruining it for myself just sucked. That's what made me finally realize I had to deal with my baggage.

Our emotions show us what we *really* want. They also show us what we *really* do not want. The problem is we get so caught up in our emotions that we don't get down to the problem or the lesson. Then it festers and grows and becomes this trauma that we let follow us into our grave. We become so consumed by triggers that we lose our true self.

How do we find our way back to ourselves? Forgiveness.

I'm talking about accepting the past so you can drop off that sack of sad.

Here's what happened to me. I jumped into a toxic relationship after a devastating break-up because I wanted to be loved. I trusted him as if I'd known him for my whole life. The list of his wrongdoings is long, so I will shorten it as much as I can, but he ended up stealing my laptop, skates, hair dryer, and two nice watches; taking my spare car key and racking up $700 in parking tickets before crashing my car; and finally defrauding my bank accounts for $70k. After all this, I met his other girlfriend.

When I finally put it all together, I felt like I got hit by a train a million times in a row. He showed no remorse, and he actually blamed me for "burning his only bridge that he had." I absolutely hated him.

After the loss of so many things, mainly my sanity, I became sort of a loose cannon. I cried so hard about things that it just didn't make sense to cry about. That was when my amazing, talented, smart, and beautiful mother brought to my attention the fact that I was allowing bad feelings to fester. This was leading me toward another deterioration of my mental health, which had already taken a huge hit. It was a classic tale of a double down, and I don't mean the burger.

I was festering. Okay, so what? What did I do? What can any of us do to fix this clearly important problem? I used four main steps that I will share, but first there are a few things we need to understand.

Forgiving someone for a past trauma is downright difficult. It's super-duper hard. When you're going through the steps to let go of bad emotions and come back to your true self, remember that you will not get it right the first time. You probably won't even get it right the tenth time. But through the sum of all your tries, you will eventually release the poison and even turn it into a blessing.

We do *not* forgive someone for them. You don't have to see their face ever again or even tell them that you've forgiven them if you don't want to. We forgive for ourselves. Our sanity. Our soul. We forgive because we want to grow past that unfortunate situation, and maybe because we want to shove our success in the face of our depression. We forgive because if we don't we will succumb to a lifetime of triggers that will ruin our holidays, beautiful places, and precious moments.

Last of all, you need to forgive until it is within you. This means if you're going to forgive someone, if you're going to choose a life that's amazing and beautiful, then commit to it and do not half-ass it. Really stick it to "the man" or whomever, and at a certain point you won't ever have to look back and feel sad.

It wasn't easy, trust me, but I finally realized how right my mom was. Facing your toughest battles is not fun. It's so much easier to pretend they don't exist. The problem is the more you keep pretending your battles don't exist, the more the universe will give you reminders that they do. Maybe we drink a little too much and freak out over essentially nothing, maybe we get triggered by someone we love and ruin a relationship, or maybe we honestly just feel bad about way too many things. Whatever your situation is, remember that it is possible to get through these things. We can't control what happens around us, but we can control what happens within us. Allowing ourselves to no longer be the victim and taking control is the most empowering feeling. Taking that first step to deciding that you're going to deal with it will do wonders. Sometimes the hardest part is recognizing we have stuff to deal with, but making the choice to change changes you. I will never forget how amazing it felt to finally start sorting out my baggage, and I will never pick it up again.

Here's what I did to finally let go of my baggage:

1. Cry. Talk. Listen to as much sad music or watch as many sad movies as you want. Punch a punching bag, for crying out loud, if that's how you get out your anger. However you do it, you have to find a way to let the emotions out. Just make sure you do not hurt anyone else in this process, as much as you might think it would help.

2. I like to call this step "the neutralizer" because it neutralizes your trauma. Take a notebook and write down every single negative thing about your situation. Don't stop even if you're bawling your eyes out. Keep writing until something inside says stop, and not a second before. Honestly, this is my least favorite step because you really have to think, really submerge yourself into those awful feelings you don't want to feel. You'll likely be exhausted after this, so once you're done, put the notebook aside for the rest of the day and do something nice for yourself.

    The next day, take out your notebook and write down all the positive things about the situation — outcomes, events, people, or memories. Just write down anything and everything that makes you feel fuzzy inside. In my case, I wrote out how my situation made me go home and be shown so much love from my mother. I also wrote down all the lessons I learned, including what I now knew about how people can be and what to do with money. When you are finished, put your book away. You can burn it or if you're feeling a little less pyro today, just hide it. There is no need now to look back at it. You have seen all the bad and all the good, and you do not have to relive any of it anymore.

3. The hard work is over for the most part. The last step helped you balance your emotions. It may take a little while to set in, maybe even a few months, but eventually you will be able to think about the situation clearly. This third step is for when you reach that point, when you can put your emotions aside and look at different perspectives. For example, if someone stole from you, you can find ways to give them the benefit of the doubt. Imagine your story as a Hollywood movie — maybe they had to take your phone to save someone's life. That kind of thing. Play the understanding game.

    If you're still feeling very emotionally up and down, go back to step two until you're able to step back from your emotions fully. Once you remove emotions from any given situation, different perspectives and understandings will become clear because you are no longer biased toward a specific outcome.

4.   The fourth step is a big one, and you may have to repeat it multiple times depending on how many wrongs you need to let go. This is the forgiveness step. It takes the least amount of time, a mere few sentences, but it is ultimately the most impactful. Some of the forgiveness statements I used included: "I am in the right place at the right time. The things that are happening are happening for the lessons I must learn; they are just things, and I am now free to let them go." Get specific with your forgiveness statements. If it is the person you want to forgive, then allow yourself to say, "I forgive (insert name here). They didn't know any better as they have not been shown the love I have in my life."

As I said before, you do not forgive for someone else. You only need to say these things out loud to yourself. This step will help you release those negative emotional blocks. You can change your mantra from day to day, focusing on different aspects of the hurt and releasing them. Just promise me that you will embrace these like your life depends on it! The lighter, happier you is depending on you.

Forgiveness is not for other people. We do it for ourselves. Once you get through the emotions like the angst and the stress, the trauma becomes just another situation. When you're in the thick of it, remember that the light is not just at the end of the tunnel — it's all around you as well. Open your eyes and find even the smallest thing to be thankful for. For me, it was my mother's unwavering support. Find what you're thankful for, and just feel that gratitude. Feel gratitude for yourself and for the fact that you've taken steps to help yourself. When we do that, we are ultimately loving ourselves, so as you are moving slowly through these steps be proud of your badass self!

These steps took me about a year and a half to get through, so don't feel rushed. All will happen in its own time; you and only you will know when you are okay. And just so you know, it is okay *not* to be okay. There is not one person in the entire world who doesn't have struggles; it is how you deal with them that makes you stronger. The people who have had the biggest struggles can handle bigger ones. At some time, everybody faces a catastrophe. It's like school — you get through one test only to face a harder one. The truth is that there will always be something tough around the corner, but there will also be something *amazing* to go along with it. What are you willing to get past in order for something great to happen?

Without all this nonsense, life would be boring. Life would be easy and dull, and we wouldn't appreciate a darn thing. If we never had the bad relationships, how on earth would we understand when we have a good one? None of us ever want to find ourselves in a bad situation, but sometimes we need to experience pain to grow. Do me a favor and look back at a bad situation from a long time ago, one that no longer hurts you. Are you stronger because of it in some way? If you think hard enough, you'll likely say yes.

Life is about growing, and if we aren't doing that, then we're just dying. If you don't believe me, then picture your life in five years. What if you had the same income, friends, job, baggage, and belongings that you have today? Nothing has changed in that five years — you haven't learned anything, and you have the same stuff. Sounds boring, doing the same thing with the same things. I don't know about you, but in five years, I would at least like a new car and some new clothes.

It wasn't easy to get over that destructive relationship. It was extremely painful, it led me to hurt people around me, and it seemed to be an awful gift that just kept giving. However, it also led me on one of the most rewarding journeys. The person I've become, the things I've learned, and the goals I'm going to accomplish now are priceless. I could never have done any of it if it weren't for my ex taking everything I thought I had away from me. He made me grow and work on myself, and now I can try to help other people going through the same thing. That alone is worth every horrible second of wrenching heartbreak.

Wherever you are in life, whatever you're going through, trust me when I say it's going to be all good. It worked out exactly how it should have, even if you hate exactly how that was. We need your future, we need your wisdom, and there are people waiting for you to help them, too, so get to it! Follow these steps and *drop that baggage off*. It no longer serves you, and you know that. *You are so worth it. You are a divine being. You can get through this.*

I MAKE MYSELF PROUD.

CHAPTER 4

Lessons of Love

"F.E.A.R. has two meanings. Forget Everything And Run or Face Everything And Rise. The choice is yours."
~ Anonymous

BY: CARLEY INGLIS

Carley Inglis

https://clearlylearningsolutions.com

ig: @clearly_carley | fb: @Clearly-Consulting

CARLEY IS A SOCIAL BUTTERFLY. Her perfect place is somewhere on a beach in the sun and sand, surrounded by great people. She enjoys spending time building strong and lasting relationships and learning from those in her life.

In 2017, Carley left her corporate career where she was a manager of learning and development and founded Clearly Learning Solutions. She has since supported larger retailers such as TJX Canada and Holt Renfrew, but works primarily with small startups, not-for-profits, and independent retailers on program design and delivering learning modules to set them up for success. Carley is an expert facilitator and prefers working with groups in classroom and workshop settings. She is regarded as one of the best in retail for her ability to design workbooks to set employees up for success to execute all areas of standard operating practice.

Carley is also an avid volunteer. Almost as important to her as her two dogs, she volunteers regularly and in a variety of ways. From chairing her board of directors to volunteering in bottle, food, and toy drives, to spending weeks in the summer at camps for children with cancer, she believes giving back is the least she can do for having such a great life.

Carley lives her life by two simple rules: keep things simple and "it is none of your business what people say behind your back" and she believes that these two things help her keep living her best and happiest life!

I AM A FIRM BELIEVER in the expression "what you don't know can't hurt you." In some scenarios, ignorance *can* be bliss. Sometimes having knowledge of a thing causes you more pain than not knowing it. But what if learning what you don't know could actually help you, or possibly even change your life? This is where my journey starts. I'm not going to tell you about how I found my great romantic love but rather how I found my love for me. Essentially, I had to lose love in order to find my love for life and myself. Sometimes we need to bring light to what is in the dark in order to find out who we really are and what we are made of.

I was raised to be very strong, and I became incredibly self-sufficient at a young age. I was, and still am, "one of the boys." I drink beer, watch sports, enjoy being outdoors, go camping and ATVing, and I take care of my house and car. I pretended to be okay with being the best friend instead of the girlfriend. I thought I was okay with sex with no strings attached. I pretended as if my feelings were never hurt and as if it took nothing for me to play the strong card and just move on. As a result, my relationships were either short-lived (to the point where I almost convinced myself there was something wrong with me) or emotional roller coasters. Through all of them, I tried to convince myself that I was okay with things when I actually was not. Truth is, I was never okay with any of that. I was just trying to be a version of myself that I thought the men in my life wanted me to be.

When I was in my teens, I went through a typical "I hate everything" phase. I didn't like my school because most of my friends were in different schools and I felt alone. I had acne and a bad haircut, and I had developed a really unhealthy relationship with food. This was when I really started dimming myself to become what other people wanted me to be. I was learning that if I pretended to be confident and was the girl who got along with anyone — like a chameleon — then I would at least get attention and not feel so alone.

My first real taste of attention came from a boy named Ace. He wasn't the most attractive guy, but he was popular and nice and loved music. We had developed inside jokes during our hours of phone conversations. Then we went to our first party together, my first party ever. Our inside jokes had escalated to be a little bit on the racy side, and I loved the attention. But then came the part where we were alone and drinking, and I realized I wasn't ready. When I said no, he listened — he was a total gentleman about it. He didn't make me feel bad or feel like a loser, but come Monday everything had changed. No more attention. Now he wanted to be "just friends" and this made me feel like I needed to bury my true self even deeper.

After a while of dimming myself, though, love started to teach me some lessons.

Enter Lesson One. We will call him Joe. Joe was the first guy in a while who paid any attention to me after Ace. He didn't care that I wasn't confident or conventionally pretty. For whatever reason (which I am still not sure of to this day), he just loved spending time with me. We grew close, and I was smitten. We spent an obscene amount of time together, and this was before cell phones were really popular, so it wasn't as easy as it is now! Here was the problem: for the longest time, Joe had no idea how I felt. He was my first love, the guy I lost my virginity to, but at no point did I ever tell him that I loved him or wanted a relationship with him. Any time we crossed the line beyond friendship, we would make the excuse that we were bored or lonely or just had such a great friendship that it was easy. I never argued with any of that.

After spending six months abroad in Australia, I came home feeling like a new woman. I was ready to tell Joe how I felt and what I wanted, willing to risk losing the friendship over it. There were tears, laughter, and so many emotions floating around the room when, to my surprise, he admitted that he had always felt that way about me, too.

Later that day, his phone rang. It was a girl he had been dating while I was away — she was pregnant. And that was that.

Lesson One learned. Don't hide your feelings. Maybe telling Joe earlier would have changed the outcome and maybe it wouldn't have. But because I hid how I felt for so long, that is an answer I will never get.

Before I get to Lesson Two, it is important for you to know that I have always been a huge daddy's girl. I know a lot of people say that, but my father and I were best friends. He helped me move into my very first house, taught me how to cook and clean, how to cut the grass, and how to never stop working hard. One of my fondest memories is coming home after my four-hour daily commute from my very long day at work to a hot dinner for me and my friends before our weekly dance classes. My father knew what it meant to be a real man.

My father passed away very suddenly and unexpectedly in 2009, while I was out of the country. It was hard to survive this, but I did, on my own. My dad had raised a strong, independent, and intelligent woman, and I had learned my lesson with Joe. I was never going to be in that sort of relationship again. I knew my dad would want better for me.

Enter Lesson Two. We will call him Ryan. Ryan was *hot*, like 100 percent the most attractive guy I had ever known. He was tattooed, muscular, and reasonably tall, with perfect teeth and so much more. He checked every box on my physical checklist. I will never forget when my sister told me about him. Her exact words were, "He is really good-looking, but he likes girls like you, you know, with curves!" Looking back that makes me laugh, but at the time I was completely flabbergasted at the fact that a beautiful specimen such as Ryan could ever be interested in me. If you hadn't noticed the theme, I was severely lacking in confidence.

We got to know each other, and I fell in love pretty much instantly. Because I had learned my lesson the first time, I was very expressive about how I felt. I was the one who asked for the relationship to be more serious and exclusive, and after six months, I said "I love you" first. This time, I was not going to hold back and risk missing an opportunity.

In addition to being attractive, Ryan had a wonderful personality. He was caring, compassionate, thoughtful, hard-working, and so many other awesome things, most of which reminded me of my dad. We moved quickly-ish, and next thing I knew, we were living together.

Throughout our relationship, I pretended to be okay with his abundance of female friends, some of whom he said were his best friends. I pretended to be okay with him leaving a gathering to spend an hour on the phone consoling another woman. I pretended to be okay with him going out for coffee with the woman who rear-ended him instead of calling to tell me where he was after saying he got in a car accident.

Let's get to the point — I knew he was cheating. But at that time, I was of the mindset that what you don't know can't hurt you (boy, was that wrong!) and that if you didn't know for sure, you had no reason to be mad.

Part A of Lesson Two: I learned to *always* trust my gut, which has led me to be so proud of the person I am today. No matter how many times Ryan called me crazy or told me that he didn't have time to cheat even if he had been that type of guy, I couldn't get that nagging feeling to go away. I should have listened.

Despite eventually learning that my instincts were correct, I truly believed that forgiveness was necessary for me to move on, so I let it go. We reconnected, and I welcomed him back into my life. My trust issues fell away. This started four years of me convincing myself that I was comfortable with him cheating on other women with me — after all, I wasn't in the dark this time. I believed that his lies weren't a big deal because I wasn't the one doing something wrong. Whenever I acknowledged how I was feeling and shared it, he would then start to pretend.

Pretend he was still in love, pretend to care, pretend he had remorse over how we had gotten to that place. I will spare you all the details of our four-year crazy, toxic, emotional, hurtful, bad karma-riddled disaster-fest. What I will say is that forgiving him was not an option.

After our last blowout, when I had finally had enough and stood up for myself, I realized that forgiveness was something I didn't need to give and something he didn't deserve. I needed to forgive myself for staying, and honor that I was a good person in his life when he was reflecting pain onto me that he needed to deal with on his own. It wasn't about me.

Lesson Two, Part B. Doing what I need to be happy and okay with myself may not mean doing what is best for everyone else. If forgiveness isn't good for me at a certain point, then too bad, I'm not going to give it. I often remind myself that my dad would always want me to do what is best for me.

Why was it okay for him to lie? Call me crazy? Knowingly hurt me and others? And on top of that, why did I deserve any of that? Why did I accept it and feel I owed him forgiveness? Lesson Two learned.

I do not harbor any ill feelings toward either Joe or Ryan. I learned important lessons and I wish them both great lives. In fact, I even still call one of them a friend. After all, thanks to them, I developed the confidence I need to know what I want and not settle for less. I learned that what you don't know *can* hurt you because when you don't know, you can't learn and grow. If I had learned to trust my gut and be confident earlier on, I could have spared myself a lot of heartache. My heart wanted to love, and so it did. But it is through that heartache I found my real love — I love myself. I learned enough to know better when things don't feel right. I learned enough to be confident in my decisions, about the people I spend time with and countless other things. I learned enough to know that even though it sometimes hurts, there is always a lesson to be learned — and those lessons are often the most beautiful.

This book is all about love and the various forms in which it shows up in people's lives. I hope that you can feel that sometimes the biggest way to experience love is through heartbreak. Through the loss of a loved one, whether it be a friendship, a romantic relationship, or a family member, we can experience growth, transition, and some of the most profound moments in life. And sometimes, when you love someone enough to let them go, you make room for some of the biggest love you'll ever experience: love for yourself.

Dear Love,

Thank you for the lesson.

I GIVE MYSELF PERMISSION TO RECEIVE THE LOVE,

RESPECT, LOYALTY, COMPASSION, ABUNDANCE, HEALTH,

PEACE, AND HEALING THAT I DESIRE.

I GIVE MYSELF PERMISSION TO RELEASE

WHAT NO LONGER SERVES ME.

IT'S SAFE TO LET GO,

IT'S SAFE TO RELEASE, AND

IT'S SAFE TO MOVE FORWARD.

CHAPTER 5

Do Teenagers Ever Learn How to Love Themselves?

"What would it look like if our children loved themselves just a little bit more?"

BY: ROBERTA FERNANDEZ

Roberta Fernandez

ig : @aspacetopause | fb: @roberta.gomez.mft | tw: @aspacetopause

ROBERTA FERNANDEZ IS A wife, daughter, sister, author, teacher, counselor, psychotherapist, consultant, and woman of color. Roberta is the founder of A Space to Pause Psychotherapy Practice in South Pasadena, CA. She received her undergraduate degree in business administration from UC Riverside in 2000 and her master's of science in clinical psychology in 2012. Since then, she has become a psychotherapist who enjoys working with people of all ages. She has been working in Catholic school settings for five years as a counselor, which has provided her a unique opportunity to assist children and teenagers with improving their social and emotional well-being. Roberta is passionate about nurturing children's souls by introducing them to the basics of self-love and the use of meditation and mindfulness practices. Roberta started meditating at the age of nine and now teaches meditation individually and in the classroom to students in pre-k through eighth grade. Roberta is also a consultant for businesses looking to improve morale and relationships within their work environments.

Roberta is passionate about learning about cultures different than her own. She has been a missionary with Mustard Seed Communities in Jamaica and San Lucas Tolimon in Guatemala. Roberta enjoyed visiting and living within these communities to absorb, learn, and coexist in their cultures and traditions.

Roberta loves to bring humor and laughter wherever she goes and to have fun! She loves to travel, do yoga, attend spin class, write, and visit meditation studios wherever she goes, and she enjoys dreaming, traveling, creating, and learning in her spare time. She is constantly in search of ways to grow, learn, and get the most out of her life. She recently took an acting class for fun and enjoys trying new activities that involve adventure.

RECENTLY, I HAVE BEEN TALKING with the adolescents and teenagers I work with about what it would look like if they loved themselves just a little bit more. What would it look like if they knew ways to love themselves more actively, or to treat themselves more lovingly? These questions have led to discussions about how much they dislike themselves, how much they care about what others think of them, and how in the world we can figure out how to love ourselves. Adolescents and teenagers are constantly in spaces where everyone in their world is trying to mold them in some way, and they are completely aware of it. They're taught how to get As in school, how to become better athletes, how to manage their time well, how to make new friends, how to be assertive, how to manage social media, how to ignore distractions, how to be good people, how to get into college, how to manage anxiety, depression, suicidal thoughts, homicidal thoughts, and more. These are very important skills, but do we ever teach them how to be compassionate with themselves through one of the most difficult times in their life?

How can we foster self-love and compassion in a teenager who is lacking this component of their mental health and well-being? Whether you are a teacher, coach, parent, counselor, or someone else who has an influence in a child's life, you have an important opportunity to discuss self-love and self-care. It is by having this conversation about self-care and how we as adults pay attention to our own self-care that we can truly impact our children for years to come. We can teach our children how to love themselves, how to have compassion when they fall short, and how to take control of the areas in their life they have control over. We can teach children to look at self-love creatively and to have fun, explore, and experiment with improving their self-care. Self-care can then help them experience less anger and irritability, increase their mental well-being, improve their relationships with parents and peers, develop their ability to face adversity with grace and dignity, and maybe even help them experience love of self, possibly for first time in their lives.

Teenagers have so much to learn already. Does asking them to learn to love themselves more just add one more thing to their plate? When I asked this, one teenager replied, "Yes, but I think it's necessary." I think she was right. Adolescents and teenagers have many bids for their attention in this world. The Netflix series *13 Reasons Why* provides what I think is an accurate example of how all the pressures in a teenager's life can lead to self-destruction or bleed over into depression and anxiety for years to come. I think it's worth it if one of their options instead is to figure out how to love themselves more.

When I was growing up, I had what they call a "tiger mom." Even now, as I write "tiger mom," I feel a sense of pride that she was "hard" on me. Her motto was, "If you want to succeed at something, you have to *practice* outside of practice." I agree with this mindset, and I have realized it has played a large part in my drive and work ethic, including my passion to own my business, my courage to write, and my desire to serve my community. Essentially, I learned how to hustle. As I have gotten some experience under my belt as an adult woman working with teenagers, I have also realized that sometimes this drive has come at the cost of my mental health.

As a kid, I experienced what my parents normalized as "nerves." They implicitly communicated that everyone experiences this from time to time. I recall waking up to my mother vomiting before we traveled to her hometown. I never knew this was due to anxiety and fear. I just thought it was "nerves." As a child, I had no reason to mind or question her behaviors. And at nine years old, I replicated the behavior, vomiting before my karate tournaments. They terrified me, and I was extremely anxious. I worried about having the wind knocked out of me, which happened often. My behavior was normalized as "just nerves." The words "self-care" and "self-love" were not in most family vocabularies in the '70s and '80s. There was no discussion about how to love or take care of oneself or to recognize one's needs.

I relied on my parents to know what was best for me. They did the best they could, given their own upbringing. Unfortunately, a generation of ingrained behaviors ultimately led to self-neglect and lack of self-love. All in all, my childhood had its fair share of ups and downs, as do many. I had a reason to have severe anxiety, with a father struggling from the disease of alcoholism, a mother trying to raise her two children essentially alone, and the constant feeling that I needed to achieve more in order to be okay. Because my childhood anxiety was normalized, I thought it was okay to ignore my own needs. As an adult, I struggled with not being able to ask for what I need: everything from requesting a monetary raise at work, making a change in jobs, putting an end to unacceptable behavior, saying no to drugs and alcohol when I wanted to, speaking up to friends and family, taking risks, saying no to requests that didn't feel right, trusting myself to end poor relationships, sticking up for others who were being treated poorly, resting when I need to rest, taking a day off, giving myself a chance to mourn, or being in a relationship without losing myself. All of these are acts of active self-love that I struggled to perform because I just didn't learn how.

I was twelve years old. My family knew it was the day I would be awarded my black belt, but I didn't. I had the flu and I felt very weak, sick, and exhausted. I felt a sense of betrayal when my parents told me I had to go to karate practice anyway. I remembered thinking, very dramatically, *Even if I am dying, I still have to go to practice?* This was one of my first memories of being powerless over my parents' control over me.

It was awful. Even though I was only a child, I sensed strongly that I needed to stay home and get well. But the cognitive message I received that evening was to ignore and push down my needs and do what I said I would do at the cost of my physical and mental health. And so I did, that day and for years after. Even in relationships, I did not allow myself to have needs, wants, dreams, desires. I kept those to myself.

The lack of self-love, respect, and acceptance developed during childhood left a mark, one that led me to ignore my needs, stay small, and not create any waves. This was through no fault of my parents'. They felt they were doing what was best for me and they were excited for me on the day I received my black belt, but this event highlights the importance of evaluating the messages we may send our children about self-care and sports, education, extra-curricular activities, and friends. Are you proud of them for pulling an all-nighter because you feel they have the drive to succeed in school? At what cost? Are you okay with them attending practice even if they are ill or unwell because just because you want them to play in the next game? Do you know if they will fit in more if they attend a friend's birthday party, or if they stay home recovering from the flu?

In order for teenagers to learn to love themselves more actively, they first need to be interested in and motivated to accept themselves. We must accept ourselves before we can *love* ourselves. Adolescents and teenagers are trying to develop confidence. Parents, teachers, and coaches can help provide tools, tips, and ways to go through this process with more ease and love. Some conversation topics that can lead to insightful reflection for our adolescents and teenagers include learning to love themselves for who and where they are in life, giving themselves a chance to reflect on and celebrate their accomplishments big and small, recognizing a time when they stood up for a person getting bullied, highlighting a time they invited the least popular kid to their birthday party or complimented another person's style, apologizing to someone when they were wrong, being honest when it's not in their best interest, and standing up for what they believe in even if it's not popular. These all represent areas in a teenager's life in which they can build character and real, not false, pride. This is a great place to start to teach teens to love themselves just a little bit more than they already do, just a little more actively.

Teenagers can also build a sense of self and character by engaging in spiritual practices (yes, teenagers are spiritual, too). Such practices can include sitting in silence, meditating, practicing mindfulness, taking part in a group, and acknowledging and accepting their strengths and weaknesses.

Through my life experiences, my later work with adolescents and teenagers, and my research, I've identified what I think are the bare necessities for mental health. I've also come up with six tips to help you and your child along the journey of self-love. Together, these are tips you can walk away with to treat yourself more lovingly, to love yourself just a little more actively, and to discuss mental health and self-love with any adolescent/teenager whom you counsel, teach, parent, coach, or tutor.

Research shows that for the most optimal well-being, an adolescent/teenager needs a minimum of three meals and two snacks, eight to ten hours of sleep, and thirty minutes of exercise daily. If these basic needs are not being met, it can often be mistaken for deeper issues, such as learning disorders, anxiety disorder, and ADHD. For example, a child who is not eating breakfast every morning because they are "not hungry" may display symptoms of anxiety, worry, or fidgety behavior in the classroom. Parents or teachers may then ask this child to get assessed based on their "hyperactivity" and they may end up meeting the criteria for ADHD.

Parents and caretakers can act to ensure children's optimal brain and mental health. For example, a child can speak with a school counselor to discuss the benefits and consequences of proper eating, exercise, and sleep habits. If your child cares about their test scores and grades, this can be a great motivator for improving their knowledge of how the brain works and increasing their understanding that they have control over their own decisions. Not only can this improve accountability and responsibility, it can also improve teenagers' self-compassion and self-esteem by establishing a sense of ownership of their well-being. These improvements will then trickle over into their college and adult life.

Research also shows that when you learn how to manage stress and ask for help, your potential health risks, including mental health risks, decrease. I have had young adults in my counseling office admit to feeling overwhelmed by the demands and responsibilities they face, and to their lack of knowledge of how to take care of themselves. Students do not have to suffer, pull all-nighters, or take drugs to stay up just to pass a test or complete a project. This leads me to my six tips to help you or your child in the journey of self-love and self-compassion.

1. Planning and Organizing vs. Procrastinating

Based on the experiences of the many adolescents and teenagers I have seen in my office over the years, procrastination often leads to anxiety and depression. Procrastination and I are also great friends. For much of my life, I held the false idea that I do my best work when under pressure. However, if "doing my best" is just another way of saying, "I got it done," is that really my best?

Planning and organizing with love are an antidote to procrastination. A fun way to manage procrastination is to plan and organize with friends. Friends can help hold us accountable for our responsibilities, as well as for planning self-care, fun, and adventure into our calendars.

There are many ways for parents and teachers to find support and guidance for children struggling with procrastination. Several excellent books on the topic include *The Perfectionism Workbook for Teens: Activities to Help You Reduce Anxiety and Get Things Done* by Anne Marie Dobosz[3] and *Overcoming Procrastination for Teens: A CBT Guide for College Bound* Students by William J. Knaus.[4] You can also inquire whether your child's school has a counselor who can help expand their knowledge of how to manage their mental health and well-being. Outside counseling with a licensed mental health professional such as a Licensed Marriage & Family Therapist, a Licensed Clinical Social Worker, or a psychologist can also provide treatment plans to reduce symptoms of anxiety and procrastination or to improve the management of life stressors and challenges.

2. Laughter and Fun

I have had countless adolescents and teenagers share with me the difficulty they face when it comes to scheduling some free time or relaxation into their day. There is so much pressure to say the right thing, do the right thing, study the right way, feel this way, don't feel that way, or get into this high school or that college, that teenagers often feel that having fun is wrong if they are not getting straight As, are behind on homework, or if they are just struggling socially with family or friends. Most teenagers have so many commitments in their daily schedule that if they do have downtime, they experience feelings of guilt and laziness. This is a fast way to create workaholics at a very young age. Luckily, there is an easy fix. Free time, including one to three hours of no homework, is a must for our children's mental health and clarity. We live in a culture that praises performance, but it cannot come at the cost of our children's mental health. The ability to manage stress at this young age is vital to teenagers' future well-being. We need to make sure that our teenagers have time for just breathing and being — which leads me to the next item on my agenda for self-care and teenagers.

3.   Mindfulness

I have had the pleasure of teaching mediation and mindfulness tools to children as young as four and as old as thirteen. Children crave mindfulness. Whether it is meditating before a big test, mindfully breathing throughout the day, or mindfully walking from class to class, incorporating mindfulness and meditation into children's daily routine is a game changer. According to UCLA's Mindful Awareness Research Center, "[m]indful awareness can be defined as paying attention to present moment experiences with openness, curiosity, and a willingness to be with what is."[5] Mindfulness can improve self-esteem, minimize self-consciousness and insecurity, improve empathy, and increase a sense of being a part of a community with classmates. Teenagers and adolescents tend to do mindfulness well, but their natural inclination may not be nurtured or encouraged in the home or at school. In both environments, there may be the sense that there is no time to sit for five minutes because the schedule doesn't allow for it. Luckily, mindfulness has become a buzzword in today's society, and there are increasing opportunities to improve the school and home environments by incorporating mindfulness practices. I love the *Calm* and *Headspace* apps, and there are also many mindfulness workshops for teenagers, including UCLA's Mindful Awareness Research Center and the Spirit Rock Retreat Center in Northern California.

4.   Physical Health

"My child has anxiety every time he is getting ready to go to school. There must be something happening at school. What do you think it is?" I have often received this message from parents concerned about whether their child is being bullied, excluded, or treated poorly. It is true that complaints of a stomachache or headache commonly stem from stress and anxiety, but this is not always the case. Students may be suffering from a stomach flu, constipation, viruses, acid reflux, h pylori, hyperthyroid, hypothyroid, or something else. Before assuming that a child's physical problems stem from mental health challenges, the first step in addressing symptoms should always be a visit to their pediatrician for a full physical exam. This will rule out any physical issues that can be managed with medicine and could help your child thrive symptom-free.

5.   Emotional Health

This is a part of our mental well-being we often overlook as parents, educators, coaches, and mentors. Emotional health includes setting boundaries, resolving conflict healthily, making and keeping friends, learning how to let go of unhealthy friendships, and knowing how and when to ask for what you need from parents and caregivers, teachers, or the school. Emotional health also includes finding the right time to speak up when presented with unacceptable behaviors and how to say no when you feel in your gut that you do not want to do something. Finally, there is also emotional safety. This means being able to talk with an adult who "gets it," which is crucial when a teenager is going through difficult feelings or situations. Many children have shared with me their lack of trust in sharing big feelings with certain people, which is clearly a lack of emotional safety. When your child is struggling, they need to have someone with whom they feel emotionally safe to share their most intimate and difficult struggles. Emotional safety leads to healthy self-esteem and increased well-being.

6.   Screen Time

Snapchat, Twitter, Instagram, texting, group texting, FaceTime, tagging, reposting, unfollowing, following, DMing — whoa! If that list overwhelms you, it's not your fault. There is so much pulling at teenagers' peace of mind. Many children go to sleep with their electronic devices, resulting in late night group chats, FaceTime, and video gaming at all hours of the night. Our children have alerts going off on their phones at one in the morning from a friend in crisis who needs attention. Many parents struggle with how to manage their children's electronic devices — *Screenagersmovie.com* is an amazing resource to help parents and educators navigate the demands that screen time has placed on our children.

The innate ability to care for one's self and to develop self-compassion is vital to teenagers' mental health and physical health. This includes learning their basic self-care needs: eating three meals and two snacks and getting eight hours of sleep and thirty minutes of exercise every day. By learning to care for themselves, teenagers and adolescents will also nurture their future adult selves. They will be more resilient, experience less anxiety and depression, improve their ability to manage pressure and stress, and ultimately be able to enjoy life instead of engaging in the rat race of accolades, accomplishments, getting ahead, and chasing a six-figure salary at the unfortunate cost of mental health and well-being. Striving for a certain lifestyle is important, but it is more important to teach our children how to experience gratitude, peace, dignity, confidence, and enjoyment of life, regardless of their circumstances. This lifestyle will allow the difficult times to be just that: difficult but not unbearable, hopeless, or without a light at the end of the tunnel.

There is always hope in love for oneself, and that hope lies within. The most important message we can teach our children and remember for ourselves is this: *enjoy* your life — you've got one.

I AM WORTHY OF
MY OWN LOVE
AND SUPPORT.

CHAPTER 6

The Gift of Love
Begins with You

"Find yourself and nurture her, love her, despite her flaws."

By: Chelsea Forrest

Chelsea Forrest

. . . .

CHELSEA FORREST IS A Human Resources Administrator for the Royal Canadian Navy, as well as a writer, mother, wife, and surrogate. She is so excited to be completing her first written project.

Born and raised in Halifax, Nova Scotia, Chelsea now lives in Victoria, British Columbia with her spitfire daughter, the most caring husband, and three ferocious felines. In her free time, Chelsea enjoys watching horror movies, playing board games, hiking, and taking in the arts in all their idioms. She is dedicated to helping improve the lives of those around her and guiding others on their path to happiness.

IT HAS ALWAYS BEEN EASY FOR ME TO LOVE EVERYONE except for myself.

When I was twenty, I thought I knew what true love was. I couldn't have been more wrong. I ended up in a relationship typical for me at the time. It was hot and heavy. I was so in lust and so desperate for it to be love that I couldn't see what was in front of me. There were red flags right from the start, but I wanted things to work so much that I ignored them. My need to be loved and my need to be validated blinded me. If someone loved me then I could feel worthwhile. I couldn't justify my existence on my own. My value was intrinsically linked to whether or not I had a partner. Without one, I was worthless.

These thoughts and feelings are not a good way to start a relationship. We were married a short eleven months after our relationship began. I was twenty-one and he was nineteen. Neither of us was prepared. We started our marriage with no real idea of what a healthy relationship should look like, and compounded our mistake with omissions and half-truths, if not outright lies.

From the beginning, it was a tenuous affair. I was so wrapped up in the idea of marriage and what it traditionally brought that I didn't stop to think about whether I should be married. I just needed it. I felt like I couldn't be complete without it. With this idea of marriage came the consuming need for a child. I worried that I wouldn't be able to have children because my endocrine system has never worked properly. We took two years to conceive, with medical intervention.

Looking back, it's hard not to think that my struggle to conceive was more because of stress and depression than anything else. I had a job and lost it. Afterwards, I couldn't bring myself to look for another job that might improve our situation. I also found out that my husband had lied about a woman he told me was out of his life. When he was locked in the bedroom doing his work (he was in university at the time), all I could do was worry about was whether he was talking to her. I couldn't seem to find my footing, and I just kept agonizing over it all. I would never be good enough for him. I wasn't good enough to have a job. I couldn't get pregnant. I couldn't support him in his education. All I did was sleep and binge watch TV. It was a spiral I couldn't get out of. I gained weight, which affected our sex life. We had no money. It was all piling on top of us, and I couldn't see a way out.

I spent the next year in that mindset. Circumstances changed and life moved forward, and I just went with it. My husband and I were just moving from one situation to another and I was unhappy with everything, but mostly myself. The weight kept coming on, and then the comments from my husband.

"I'm not attracted to you because you have gained so much weight."

The same issue was echoed by my doctor, "You need to lose weight to get pregnant."

Deep in my bones, I felt that I would be happier if I were thinner. Maybe if I lost weight, I would be worthy of him. The hatred I felt for myself was all-encompassing.

But life continued, despite my feelings about myself. I got pregnant. My husband left school and joined the Canadian Armed Forces. I ended up taking care of our daughter on my own for the bulk of two years. Every day I tried to be a good mom, but the ways in which I wasn't enough seemed to be never-ending. Those feelings of inadequacy affected every aspect of my life. My friendships and my family fell away. My thoughts, the shadowy specters in the darkest corners of my mind, seemed like my only companions. The brightest light in my life was my daughter, this little being I brought into this world, and I was failing her. Always failing.

We had planned to move from one coast of Canada to the other. It was then I found out that despite being told repeatedly that my husband had no contact with his ex, he had in fact been communicating with her. It devastated me. We argued and agreed to go to couples' counselling when we got to the other coast, so we packed and left.

We embarked on a new life away from everything and everyone I knew. Before we even got there, I had a dream about Victoria. I dreamt of green trees lining the streets, warm breezes, and people I had only heard of. The reality was as beautiful as my dream. Things felt different there. I felt different there. It was as if this tiny seed of hope within me, which I thought had long since been sterilized, had germinated.

The problem was that while I was feeling different, my relationship was not getting better. My husband would go out, but I had trouble meeting anyone. The only people I knew were his friends, the guys he had met on his work course. We had his closest friend, Eric, over every Sunday for dinner and games. My husband, feeling guilty that he got to do things outside of the home, pushed me to go out to movies with Eric, making him more of a constant presence in my life. Eventually I made a small group of my own friends, composed of the wives of the guys my husband formed connections with at work. After a while, I rarely went a day without seeing someone. I felt like life was leveling off. The contrast between this point and where I had been felt liberating. At least, that's what I told myself.

It wasn't a bad life, but it wasn't a happy life either. The more I interacted with the other wives, the more I tried to convince myself that I was happy, but even with the change in location, and all the positives that had come with it, I still felt not enough.

I had pushed myself down for too long. I put my personality into a little corner so I wouldn't offend or create waves. In an attempt to make this commitment to my husband work, I changed almost everything about myself. Stripped bare, I would put on the affectations of what I thought my husband wanted in a wife. I adorned myself with his faith, his beliefs and morals, the image of his mother, and his musical preferences: I wore anything I felt would help keep him close. Now, in a new city with new influences and with that small bud of hope, the ill-fitting façade started to come apart.

I was starting to become the person I had been before we got married, and that was causing problems. The part of me I had wrapped up so tightly that I thought I would never see her again began to resurface. I got some of my bite back, and that was enough to try to stand up for myself even when it felt futile.

I started to really struggle with myself. I wanted to feel free but I was still being bound by those shadowy specters. I had people who wanted to know the real me, but was the real me enough? No matter how much it scared me, I had to find out. I started to meet regularly with like-minded friends. These women were drawn to the spirituality I had suppressed but had been practicing since I was small, and I wanted to teach them about it. At first, it felt like teaching was just another thing I was failing at. How do you teach someone what is in your soul? My spiritual practice was intuitive, and the knowledge I had was a culmination of oral tradition, guidance, and many hours of study over many years. It was not something easily taught. Nevertheless, this attempt at edification started to clear my eyes.

While I was finding my way spiritually and socially, I was also trying very hard not to look at my relationship. More often than not, we were angry. We were hiding hurt and resentment under fake smiles and affection that was mostly there to try to convince each other that everything was still okay. The show didn't fool those closest to me, and their mounting concern for me and my daughter became palpable. It didn't help that my heart was being pulled in another direction.

While things were becoming increasingly volatile with my husband, I was finding some solace in our friend Eric. He was the quietest person I have ever met, and I didn't know where I stood with him. He was kind and gentle, and he never once raised his voice in the three years I had known him. I had never seen him angry, but there was a deep sadness or an immense loneliness to him. It was the same kind of sadness that was in me. I recognized this sadness as a dangerous type, one that could be all-consuming and in one moment just be a shade that lingers at the edge of your vision in the next. When that kind of sadness takes its grip, it can be hard to think of going on. It makes you feel like are the most useless, the most burdensome, the most unlovable. It makes you feel less than. It was not something that I would wish on my worst enemy, let alone on this man who was so genuinely kind.

The more time I spent with Eric, the more I wanted to help him. I started inviting him to everything I could, even though I knew he had a hard time being with children and my daughter was just four. We even started to get together just to hang out when my husband was on deployment. If I had any issues with my daughter, he would wait, never judging, and always with a slight look of concern. When he was around, I felt I was listened to in a way I had never been before. When I was with Eric, my ideas and feelings were important. It was the first time in a very long time that I had felt that way. My own thoughts and feelings had been pushed to the back of my mind, save for those shadows that would sometimes be so loud that they were all I could hear or see.

I don't know what Eric would say if you were to ask him about that time. All I know is that his friendship woke me from the nightmare that my life had become. For the first time in many years, I thought I might be worth more than what my husband and I had set ourselves up with. One night, thanks to the thoughts of how his friendship had made me feel, and quite a bit of alcohol, I kissed him. It was just a quick peck on the lips — I just didn't know how else to express how grateful I was for him. It was enough to scare me. My husband had been unfaithful, but I hadn't. Nothing else happened after that, but it was enough for me to wrestle with myself. I told my husband, and he laughed it off. He told me that he and Eric would talk about it and have a good laugh when Eric brought it up. I was shaken that he took it so well. I had been a terrible person, and all he did was laugh.

I knew then that we needed to fix things before it all fell apart. Who would I be if I wasn't his wife? I couldn't do anything on my own. I would never make it. I recalled the promise he made to me before we came to Victoria and started to set up counselling for us. I had all of my ducks in a row for it. I brought it up to him and expected it to be okay; after all, he had promised. But the words out of his mouth were, "We are okay, we don't need it." I can now admit that those words were the nail in the coffin: I had been sacrificing bits of myself, trying for a year to revive a relationship that was DOA.

I didn't realize that at the time, though, so I kept on going. Eventually, I got a strange friend request on social media. At first glance, I thought it was the boyfriend of my friend's mom, whom I had just met. But the more I looked at the profile, the more uncomfortable and suspicious I became. Finally, I recognized the name as a pseudonym my husband used to create fake emails and profiles. I looked at the only other friend that this profile had — it was his ex. I don't know how that friend request happened, and my husband swore it wasn't him. Later that week when my husband came home from a deployment, I could tell something was off. That Sunday, just short of two weeks after he had said we were okay, I confronted him, and he admitted to cheating on me. That was when I finally let go, allowing myself to feel all of the things I had buried over the years.

The ensuing fight was like nothing I had ever experienced before, and hope to never have again. When it was over, I left, and moved in with friends. The transition was hard; I didn't know what to do. With my emotions still raw and open from the fight, the sadness I had tried for so long to keep at bay enveloped me. It was like I kept going back into the fire. I was burning away the layers I had put on, but I didn't know what was underneath. I didn't know how I would make anything happen. I wanted to disappear and never come back. Each day, each time I broke, I looked at my daughter and knew I couldn't let life beat me. I had to make myself and our life better for her.

I wouldn't have been able to do all I have without the support of the amazing people around me. In three short weeks, I went from having nothing to securing a job and an apartment in one of the most difficult cities in Canada to find housing. I had my friends supporting me, and I had Eric. Eric was the key: he allowed me to see that I could do it, and when I felt like I couldn't he would drop everything to be by my side.

At first, I reverted to the person I had been before I got married. I was still so wrapped up in being liked. Little by little, that person began to change. I went from a fast food job to a job as a nanny because my daughter wasn't doing well in care. She was lashing out, and who could blame her? The last few years had been hard on her. As I transitioned to that job, I also joined the Royal Canadian Naval Reserves. I put everything I had into changing my life and challenging my own expectations of myself. I started to eat better, and I lost almost one hundred pounds. I went out hiking and to the movies. I took a long time to focus on myself. I needed to show my daughter what I could be.

There were many dark moments on the path to becoming who I am. There were times when the pressure of trying to balance everything seemed too much for me. Every time I buckled, though, I had Eric to reach out to. Putting one foot in front of the other, I persevered. I finally gave myself the time to figure out who I am, and I found that person I had always dreamt of being. I had never liked myself so much — I had never loved myself so much.

I had also never felt so loved. Eric and I had been in a relationship for a little over two years when we decided it was time to move in together. We had purchased a second property together and spent as much time with one another as we could, given his rigorous deployment schedule. Life just kept getting better. I had also never seen him so happy, although he was still a little anxious at times. He had at some point decided that he would be the eternal bachelor, so it took him a while to settle into our new way of being. But happiness grows where it is planted and cared for, and it thrived in our home. We have since gotten married and bought a house that is now our home. I work full time for the Canadian Armed Forces, and we live a life that at one point I could have only imagined.

After finding so much love in my life, for myself and those around me, I now feel it is in my power to pay it forward, so I have become a surrogate. I will help another person complete their family and give them a little piece of the love that I have worked for and been given. By the end of 2019, I will be able to give the gift of love.

I want others to know that anything is possible if you learn to love yourself first, flaws and all. Don't wrap yourself in the wants, needs, or expectations of others. That trap is all too easy to fall into. Find yourself. Nurture her and love her, despite the flaws. She will lead you to happiness.

THE ULTIMATE APPROVAL OF MYSELF COMES FROM ME.

CHAPTER 7

Built on Love: What Legacy Are You Leaving?

"See and feel with love, and your heart will smile all the days through."

BY: HEATHER LEE CHAPMAN

Heather Lee Chapman

hlchealth.com

ig : @heather_lee_chapman | fb: @HLCcoaching

HEATHER LEE CHAPMAN IS A personal success coach with over a decade of experience helping individuals live their best lives through mindset, movement, and nutrition. She is a certified nutritional practitioner with a diploma in applied nutrition and a personal trainer specialist. Heather has a bachelor's degree (with honors) in human kinetics, with a major in movement science and minors in biology and social sciences. She is a lifestyle and brand ambassador for Arbonne, an affiliate for the Proctor Gallagher Institute, creative director of HLChealth.com, and an inspiring educational speaker.

Heather believes we are all meant for greatness and for fulfilled and happy lives, and her mission is to ensure we all live such lives. Heather believes it is essential to treat the person as a whole — mind, body, and soul. She has helped many people, from athletes to people with brain and spinal injuries, to improve their quality of life, and she can help you to identify areas of improvement to reach your optimal physical and mental performance, identifying limiting beliefs and replacing them with affirmations and actions that serve you, thus recreating yourself to align with your truth. She can assist you to step into your power, identifying your true passion and purpose and what you are truly here to do.

LOVE AT FIRST SIGHT

A Poem
It was love at first sight, when these two souls met.
Times were rough, but they hadn't seen the best yet.
They decided they would travel to the far away land.
Here they would make money, they had a plan.
In five years, they would return,
To take care of their family with all that they'd earned.
Karl travelled first to pave the way.
Hilde would follow, she knew he would be there to greet her, she would say.
And there he was, her handsome prince, waiting for her in this far away land.
They would stick together, they had a plan.

They began their family, two beautiful girls.
They loved each other in this crazy new world.
When the time came the dollar was low.
It made no sense to return, it was a no go.
They sent money home to their family and visited when they could.
A life they were building doing all that they could.

They would work together.
Hilde would take care of the children and home.
They would buy some land, some to rent and one of their own.
Hilde would manage all on her own, the payment of the rentals, the children, house and home.
Karl would work long days providing for his family, he knew that he could.
He created businesses and provided others with work, again doing all that he could.

He was a brilliant and strong man.
A hardworking man, that knew how to do all that he can.

On this land of their own, chicken and kittens, love and fun.
Soon there would be three and they had a son.
Karl, he painted and made houses a home.
He loved this family, his wife and children of his own.
He taught them to be good people, to care for the world and to
be kind.
He was so bright, oh such a brilliant mind.

A man so strong in mind and morals.
He would lead the way from his past out of sorrows.
The head of the family as it grew.
Three became six, their children started anew.
Six became eight and eight became eighteen.
This incredible family so strong and built on love, would stick to-
gether as their mentors above.

Family first, Grandpa would say, we stick together, love is the way.
He couldn't stay forever, but in our hearts he will remain.
This brilliant and kind man, who brought us all to this far away land.
So we could live a life of freedom and love.
To have the gift of family given from above.
Karl and Hilde, love at first sight.
They brought us all here, they are our guiding lights.
To stand for the good of all.
To live in love and never fall.
And to always be grateful for all.

Blessed may we be.
It all started with their family of three.
Now it is still growing.
Karl's passion and love always showing.

The Legacy of Love

The poem above is the legacy of my late grandfather, Karl. This is the love story
of my grandparents. My grandmother, Hilde, came to Austria as a refugee from
Yugoslavia after World War Two. It wasn't an easy journey. From a well-off life,
she left everything to flee with her family for their safety. A lovely elderly couple

welcomed my grandmother, her sisters, and her mother, while her brother and father stayed somewhere else. Soon afterwards, a young gentleman arrived at the elderly couple's apartment. He, too, lived at the apartment, where he rented a room during the week while he worked in Vienna. That day, he came home from work to find that the room he was renting now housed almost an entire family. This is where my grandparents first met. The young gentleman was my grandfather. He stayed at the apartment, sleeping in the room with the elderly couple. Soon my grandfather and grandmother fell in love and decided to venture to Canada to make money, before returning home to Austria to live a better life.

My grandfather, Karl, first came to Canada with my grandmother's brother. My grandmother, Hilde, had lent my grandfather the money for the boat to Montreal. He arrived and began working to save money to send back to my grandmother, who joined him shortly after. They began their life here in Canada in 1954. They came with no money, no ability to speak the language, and just one suitcase, risking everything to create a new life for themselves and their families. About five years after arriving, as long as they thought they would stay before returning home, they decided that the cost of living in Austria was too high. Moving back home no longer made sense.

Karl worked hard to save money to send Hilde and the children home to see the family, but he never returned to Austria himself. They worked hard to save money to purchase their first home. Karl always said, "You will never get rich from your wages." He would only spend money on the necessities in order to invest in real estate so it could work for the family in the long term. Eventually, they had enough to own a rental property and a chicken farm, where they lived. The chicken farm was on a beautiful hilltop at Keele Street and Major Mackenzie Drive in Maple, Ontario. This area is now developed and looks nothing like it did at that time. They continued to save and work hard raising three children until they retired happily in their perfect home.

Karl always set an example to stand for the less fortunate and instilled that lesson upon me. He always wanted me to create a good life for myself, remind-ing me to be smart with my money, work hard, and stand up to the wrong in the world. He would study politics all day, and we would have debates about what was occurring in the world. I would play devil's advocate just to get him going — he was passionate and knowledgeable. He would always say, "You and the youth need to riot in the streets; who will make the change? This cannot go on much longer." I felt like he could have been a modern-day Robin Hood. Every chat with him contained a life lesson.

He would also always say he hoped I would find the right one to marry, because life is not meant to be spent alone.

Right before Karl passed, he told me that his quality of life was no way to live and he didn't know how much longer he could take it. He had been through things he refused to even speak of. He had lived through a war, traveled and built a life in a new country, and worked hard every day of his life doing all he could, until he couldn't anymore. He had survived a heart attack at fifty, he had felt itchy for years with no one to help him find relief, he could hardly sleep, and had just turned ninety. He was still pretty sharp, in good shape, and most definitely still passionate. He had only recently given up his driver's license, and he mostly still walked without aid, yet his quality of life was just not what he wished anymore.

The time had come, and he had decided enough was enough. The night before he passed, he told me that my grandmother hadn't been walking as much because she would stay to be with him. He noted that she loved to walk and that she was happiest when she walked. They had just celebrated their sixty-fourth wedding anniversary, and he had re-professed his love to her, apologizing if he was ever mean, telling her that he hadn't meant it and that he couldn't have done things without her. They always made a great team. Although he may have struggled in the end and was not always himself, he always wanted the best for all of us. He told me every year that his best birthday gift was my grandmother; they had married a day before his birthday. It always melted my heart.

My grandfather transitioned purposefully. No one will ever really know why, yet I have a feeling he wanted to be happy, feel good, and let my grandma be free.

I am so blessed that my grandmother is still going strong at eighty-six years old, and she has always been there for me. Hilde constantly gives me clippings on articles she finds on health and wellness. She probably moves more daily and eats more cleanly than the majority of the population. She loves going for long walks and being in nature. I love walking with her, talking with her, and learning from her. Hilde says that walking keeps her alive and that she needs the fresh air.

Hilde is my role model: she has become a stunning example of a powerful and empowered woman on her own. She has been through more than my mind could imagine, and yet she still stands here positive, moving, and caring for this incredible family. She is so strong.

My grandfather's passing had quite the emotional impact on me because he was a large part of my life. I share this because I know that death by suicide at a certain age is more common than most people think. For all those experiencing a loss, regardless of how it happened, may you find peace, gratitude, and acceptance. May you celebrate and be grateful for having them on your journey; they would want you to be happy. I am blessed to have such an amazing family and the gracious attitude that my grandparents instilled in me. I cherish all that my grandfather has taught me and the time I spent with him. We are so blessed to live in a time when women are becoming more empowered, resources are plentiful, people are awakening, consciousness is rising, and we are free to live the lives of our dreams.

I choose to see my grandfather's life as an example to follow. I choose to see the gratitude in all and leave a positive impact on this world. With gratitude may you find grace.

Leave a Legacy of Love

After the passing of my grandfather, I thought about the incredible life he led. I saw our family as his beautiful legacy: a legacy built on love. Love is really a beautiful thing. It is the one thing we all desire, isn't it? Love from a companion, love from our family, friends, and pets, love of what we do, love of what we have done.

Love is the legacy I wish to leave. I love what I do, I love what I have done, I am surrounded by incredible people whom I love so much, and I wish to leave a legacy of a family built on love. I remember my grandfather's words, "Life is not meant to be spent alone," and the quest for true love goes on.

I have learned that to find true love and happiness with another, you must first find it in yourself. What does it mean to love yourself? I think to love yourself is to know and discover yourself. To discover who you really are, your deepest desires, your deepest fears. By knowing yourself, you can love yourself exactly as you are and then use that love to create the next version of your being. When you find self-love, you wish for your own success, growth, and triumph. My triumph will leave a positive legacy, and I will be leaving it with my perfect partner as a relationship built on love.

What legacy are you leaving? Inspired by the legacy left by my grandfather, I am compelled now more than ever before to accomplish my goals, to live my truth and purpose. I wish to assist as many people as possible to live their truth as well: to live lives of joy, abundance, and fulfillment.

We are meant to be happy and free to fulfill our purpose. I once read that your purpose is to use your gift and that "your gift" means what you're best at, what makes you feel the best, and what you love the most. I know that I love to inspire others to live with intention, passion, and purpose. This is what I shall continue doing, and on a greater scale. After all, living this way myself is how I changed my self-image and gained the courage to take on my big, hairy, audacious goals.

Our self-love and our self-image determine where we are in our lives. Have you ever stopped to think, "Do I really love myself? Do my actions say that I do? Am I committed to my happiness? What makes me happy? Do I love what I do? Do I have a positive impact? What are the things I wish to do, be, and have before

I move on from this life?" I would suggest journaling and answering these questions. Through my studies and experiences, I have recreated myself many times in the last year. I am constantly setting goals and doing the work that it takes to achieve them. Once I reach one goal, I review my progress, review my big goal, revise my plan, create new base camp goals and action plans, continue with my purpose, and do it all over again. If we are not constantly evolving, we are fading away in life. It is natural selection after all: we must continue to learn and grow in order to succeed, achieve, or find fulfillment and happiness. If we don't, we perish with regrets.

But how can you accomplish all you wish if you don't love and believe in yourself? Many people have a poor self-image and don't even know it. They are constantly sabotaging their own success without realizing it. Self-love is essential. I love creating positive affirmations around the person I am becoming and I often practice them in front of the mirror. Whenever you walk past a mirror, say, "I love you," "I am healthy," "I am confident," or something positive about yourself. Really get into it. Over time, you will come to believe what you say.

Do you love and believe in yourself? If you feel like you are not where you want to be, look inside and find love. Accept yourself as you are, and as you are not. See all the good you have to offer this world. May you discover your gift, fulfill your purpose, and live in love and joy. Leave a legacy built on love as my grandfather did. Always believe in yourself, have faith in something bigger than yourself, and live in love. Think thoughts that make you feel good. Think well about yourself. Set a goal and commit to its attainment. Develop a positive and empowering self-image by using affirmations to reaffirm your worth. Louise Hay's books are absolutely filled with positive affirmations that can transform your life, and Bob Proctor and Sandy Gallagher's work will show you the way to absolute freedom, fulfillment, and success if you are willing to do the work and believe in yourself and the universe. As Bob Proctor says in his *Lead the Field* and *Thinking into Results* programs, *"You can, and you will, become what you think about,"* so think loving thoughts, love yourself, envision your dreams, and find true love.

Love starts inside you. Once you love yourself, you can project it outward fully and receive it fully. May the inspiration of my grandparents' journey and their love story show you that true love can withstand the test of time, and that we can live out our dream lives with our dream partners. You are meant to be happy. Love is the ultimate feel-good emotion; may you find love that keeps you smiling day in and day out. Don't settle — know your worth and love yourself enough to choose the right partner: someone to stand by you through thick and thin, someone to grow with you and to love you. In the end, this is your story. Write it how you wish, leave your legacy, and may you find your perfect soul mate to share your life and legacy with. As Grandpa said, life is not meant to be spent alone.

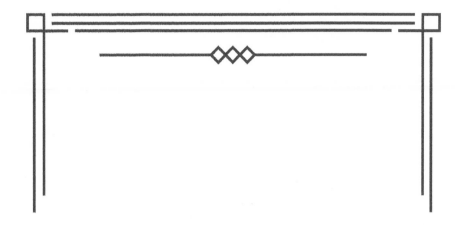

WHEN LOVE IS
THE LENS THROUGH
WHICH I SEE LIFE,
EVERYTHING IS MAGIC!

CHAPTER 8

─────

A Life of Love after Death

─────

"I could sit stale in the place I was, surrounded by sadness and self-pity, or I could make a choice to live."

By: Jess Harvey

Jess Harvey

ig: @jess_harv | fb: Jesse Roth-Harvey | tw: @jessehrv

JESS IS A DETERMINED VISIONARY with life experiences that have taught her the importance of a strong mindset. The world of writing came as a natural outlet after losing her dad and battling depression. Overcoming those years and learning how to not only manage her mental illness but also to speak publicly about it has become a passion of Jess', which serves as treatment for herself and also for those to whom she speaks. Her enthusiasm for giving back has been acknowledged by many within her community. She hopes that by sharing her story with others, she can promote greater mental health awareness.

Jess focuses now on coaching others to build confidence, promote self-awareness, and overcome boundaries in their own lives.

---

*Owning our story and loving ourselves through that process
is the bravest thing that we'll ever do.*
~ Brene Brown

FROM AS EARLY AS I CAN REMEMBER, love equaled admiration for my parents and my protectors. That love and admiration translated into hope and joy every time they looked at me, a desire to make them proud, and a constant struggle to love myself.

From a young age, love confused me, as it wears many faces and shows itself in many different ways. For example, parents can show their love for their child through happiness but also through disappointment, anger, and tears. Have you ever disappointed your parents so much that the anguished look on their faces caused you great sorrow? I guarantee their love for you never changed in those moments.

My dad was my first love: a mutual unconditional love. He saw things in me I could not see myself. Little did I know that his death would lead me down a path toward the greatest self-love I would ever know.

I had so much admiration for the way people spoke to my dad and the way they engaged with him. The friends he would make everywhere we went amazed me — he spoke to everyone! I remember thinking, *Could he possibly know that many people?* I grew to learn the answer was a definite *yes*. He took such interest in what people had to say to him, always listening intently and paying attention to the conversation. His eyes would never wander. He took a genuine interest in everyone's life — this made him someone to be admired. He had a kind of character about him that drew in a crowd and attracted people to him. A social butterfly, he could draw in a room just by entering it. We had a typical father-daughter relationship. Being the youngest child behind two brothers, our bond was clear, but to my dismay he always seemed to be the one with the upper hand.

My father and I definitely had our trying years. This is where my confusion with love came into play. Transitioning into my teenage years proved to be harder on him than it was on me. It seemed more and more common for me to see the disheartened look in his eyes and hear anger in his voice as I navigated my way through learning who I was by acting out in ways that he seemed to disapprove, yet those things never shadowed the love I knew he had for me. Love is confusing. It's messy, complicated, and crazy, all at once. All these mixed feelings can create a love that scares you because of how it makes you feel about a person. That kind of love teaches us how to love each other, or it mimics what we see in our upbringing as far as the love they give us. What we are not taught is how to love ourselves.

My struggle with mental illness began after losing my dad when I was thirty years old. After a whirlwind battle with lung cancer that seemed to last an eternity, I lost myself along with him five months to the day after they diagnosed him. My spark was gone. The wind from my sails was depleted. I became a dark, withdrawn person: someone who had lost the ability to live and love. I became so enthralled with guilt and anger (all part of the stages of grief) that I forgot how to love myself and those around me. As my daily life continued, it felt like a piece of me was buried along with him. That part of me who had a will to live was no longer present. Even though I had much to live and be present for, it was like I could not feel anything.

Imagine losing the desire to function daily. This was my painful reality, coupled with my inability to see that there was still life even after his death. Some days it was difficult to keep my head above water, and I felt as if I was suffocating.

I had to learn to live without my dad. Trying to manage a house, a business, and children and keep a marriage together all became too much for me. When mental illness takes hold, the mind becomes powerless and actions become mute. Darkness overtakes. When consumed by depression, it seems easier to turn off all emotion and focus on sadness. Using grief as my crutch and focusing on my anger and loss became my way of life for far too long. The fun, vibrant person I once was became lost in the shadow of a darker version of myself: a person unable to feel worthy of love. It's a lonely place to be — a place that no person deserves.

It took time, but once I had progressed through the stages of grief I perceived that life was continuing to go on around me even though I had felt stuck in one place. It became abundantly clear I had a choice to make: I could sit stale in the place I was in and surround myself with sadness and feelings of self-pity, or I could make the choice to live, to become a version of the image I had of my father, who I had built up highly during my lifetime. Dad was the person I had always strived to be, and to let mental illness strip that away from me suddenly seemed like a waste.

And so, the journey to love myself again began. My new path to self-awareness had to start with ways to incorporate self-love into my mental health treatment. I asked myself, "Could this work? Could I overcome my depression by learning to love myself again? Is love that powerful?"

This has been an everyday struggle during which I've had to plug into self-aware-ness and positive self-talk. I had to constantly remind and manifest to myself that in order to stay focused on the goals I had set out, I needed to learn that lov-ing myself was not conceited: it just means you know your own value acutely. Too many people give their love to someone else and lose the love they have for themselves. Others, like me, lose their ability to feel love due to a loss. It is challenging to use your energy to love yourself, but it is rewarding to regain that ability. I should have been the absolute best version of myself. I just needed the tools to see that it was possible.

I began to tap into the words of those who came before me, writing out inspi-rational quotes in my daily journal or posting them in my home for my children to see as well. As time passed, the words became my own and they proved to be an integral way to incorporate self-love back into my life. After reading them daily, those words became ingrained in me. Eventually I began to believe what I read and learned to have love for myself. I decided I wanted to be stronger than my mental illness for my own sake. I say that in the most selfless way, as my family also needed me to overcome this grief. They deserved to have me back just as much as I wanted to be back. That meant that every day, I was forced to plug into my self-awareness practice, whether or not I was feeling up to it. This practice, which has become non-negotiable, comprises speaking to myself through uplifting and motivational language, trusting my value, and never allowing the negative energy of other people affect the love I have for myself. Through this self-love practice, I've learned there is life after losing a parent. There is also life with a mental illness. My illness is no longer what defines me. For me, it's mind over matter: a practice from which I cannot waver. It took a lot of confidence to speak those words. In fact, it has taken many days, weeks, and months of repeating those exact words to myself to change my default thinking so that I could *actually* believe the words I spoke.

It has taken years of working on my mindset, but I have gotten to a point where I realize that no one else will fight this battle for me. It is my daily choice not to let this illness win. I take the good with the bad, and I learn from my shortcomings. Giving up for a day and letting the negative win puts me into a place where I am careless, unorganized, and unmotivated, and that equates to not being the best mother and wife. This happens more than I care to admit, but this is life, and a happy life takes work. If you're not making mistakes, you're not learning. I guess you could say the struggle is real.

Your happiness results directly from your effort, but they also say that things happen for a reason, even though I have had trouble believing it. I have strug-gled to comprehend what good can come from the loss of a parent resulting in a mental illness. For me, speaking out about my mental illness has become a part of my treatment plan. I used this experience to educate and motivate rather than looking at it as an impediment. These are the cards life has dealt me, and I have the choice to let them define me or to use them to shape myself. For the sake of my happiness and the happiness of those around me, it seems more fitting to continue my practice of mindfulness and to turn my energy toward being positive and loving the life I have. That is better than the alternative of letting the illness win.

I have seen the result of untreated depression. In my younger years, I had three family members take their lives because of their struggle with a mental illness. I could not understand how the end justified the means. It confused and angered me as I tried to understand what could push a person to make that final and lasting decision. How could a person not love themselves enough to stay alive? The only truth I've grown to learn is that mental illness affects everyone differently. It is not cut-and-dried, and by no means can you compare your situation to another's. One effect of depression is feeling unworthy, and when you feel unworthy you feel unlovable.

I was struggling, but to the outside world I lived the happiest of lives. I had two healthy children and a hard-working, ambitious husband. But my kids had to see me at my lowest, which is an unbearable thought most days. Instead of fearing what scars they would have from this experience, I have been open with them as I've regained my life. They will know the struggles that existed for their mom. I will not shelter them: they will see it is okay to not be okay and learn how to talk about it. In my home there will be no shame, and I will do my best to break down the stigma surrounding mental illness. My kids are my most valued treasure, and I owe it to them to be honest. It is crucial that my children know their own self-worth and the importance of loving themselves, as well as being able to openly speak about their feelings, whether they be feelings of love, sadness, or anything in between. It is important for them to know that I am not weak because of my mental illness.

It has been beneficial to my health to incorporate into my daily routine a focus on mindfulness and mindset. This practice has helped me become a much stronger, more confident mother and wife. To every person who feels defeated by a mental illness, I want to tell you that you are stronger than it is. Program your mind to push out the negative thoughts that may default and replace them with deliberate and positive thoughts

You choose your own path. Your life is a story that only you can write. It can be filled with many emotions, life-changing events, and downfalls, but it *should* be filled with as much love and happiness as you can muster up. Things happen that we don't understand, and they can make us question ourselves. You don't have to wait for life's unfortunate events to decide your worth. It is okay to love yourself. In fact, when your attitude and your energy are positive, that is when you shine the brightest.

I AM LOVED.

CHAPTER 9

True Love within Me

*"Look within, forgive yourself, and fall
so incredibly and deeply in love with
every aspect of you because loving
the queen is a true privilege. And you,
my love, are a queen!"*

By: Saira Amjad

Saira Amjad

http://sairaamjad.ca

ig: @iamsairaamjad | fb: @iamsairaamjad| | tw: @iamsairaamjad

. . . .

SAIRA AMJAD IS A PAKISTANI-CANADIAN POET, best-selling author, certified coach, entrepreneur, speaker, single mom, and self-love advocate. She came to Canada at the age of eleven and found herself bonding with art and writing as a form of self-expression. Coming from an immigrant family, she has been passionate about creating a better life.

Saira started her career at the age of twenty-one and very quickly progressed. She was at the peak of her career in project management at the time of her marriage and made a tough decision to leave her career behind to start her married life. Not too long after getting married, she found herself living in the midst of abuse and hit rock bottom.

Since then, Saira invested thousands of dollars in her personal development to learn, grow, heal, and expand in order to rebuild her life alongside her young daughter.

Her debut book, *And So She Rises*, quickly became an international bestseller on Amazon. It is a deeply intimate collection of poems about her struggle through a failed arranged marriage, a suicide attempt, sexual abuse, pressures to be "the perfect Muslim woman," and her journey to learn how to love herself.

Saira has emerged as a strong and compassionate woman who is an inspiration for men and women around the globe. As a coach, she helps women break free of the chains, embrace the goddess within, and build a fabulous empire. She strongly believes that no one should ever have to live in fear, hate, lack, abuse, or depression.

HOW DO I WRITE ABOUT TRUE LOVE

when I have not experienced it
in a very long time?

My view of true love was distorted
when I did experience it.
Now, having spent years without it
those memories seem to have faded.

I want to believe in true love;
only then could I give myself permission
to write what it feels like
to be truly in love with life
and most importantly myself.

For years I searched for love, true love, outside of myself, from others. I struggled with depression and feelings of unworthiness. As the years passed by, the pain in my chest and the knots in my stomach served as a reminder of the love-void that remained in my heart.

Growing up, I searched for the love of my father in other men. I didn't know any other children who didn't have their father with them. The money and expensive gifts we received while he lived away from us in Canada were not what I desired. I often wondered if our father loved us and if we actually mattered in his life. I wanted his time, his presence, his love, and on many occasions just a simple conversation with him. My desire to spend time with him resulted in frequent daydreaming. I dreamt of holding his hand and taking a walk to a corner store with him to buy ice cream or to the nearest plaza to buy a new outfit for Eid festivities or my birthday.

With passing time, I realized that my father would not be coming back to Pakistan and that we would be the ones to go live with him in Canada. This realization planted a new desire to hit reset on life and simply be with him. This dream came to fruition eight long years later.

> Eight years of wishing,
> hoping, praying, and
> feeling unworthy of love
> led us to Canada.

> Eight years of carrying
> heaviness in my chest.
> Eight years of suppressed
> emotions and desires.

> Eight years of anger.
> Eight years of questions.
> Eight years of guilt,
> pain, and hurt was packaged
> into my heart with care.

> At the check-in counter,
> no one saw the baggage
> I carried within me but
> rather inquired about my
> toys and belongings,
> which I left behind.

> Eight years of toys
> did not matter.
> Eight years of stuff
> were not as important
> as the memories I carried
> within me.

> Yet the life I envisioned
> was still a dream.

Immigrant fathers did not have the luxury of spending much quality time with their families back then. This reality took some time to sink in. Even while living with him, sometimes it felt like I did not matter. I craved his love while he was busy trying to make ends meet. The love I desired was present on some days, but absent on most.

I competed for my father's attention and looked for ways to earn his appreciation and approval. School was something I worked hard at. I got all the good grades and earned various awards and scholarships, for which he appreciated and praised me, but the pit in my stomach stayed with me. I did not get the love I desired, so I became resentful and my body became hyper-reactive to my thoughts and emotions. This lack of love manifested itself in various physical symptoms throughout my life, and the doctors had no explanation for it aside from stress being the common factor.

Because of my childhood programming, I believed that excelling in education and my professional life would lead me toward being loved and appreciated. I chased success and excellence for the wrong reasons, and when I acquired those things, I still felt empty and unfulfilled, so I always chased the next shining title.

I wanted a better life, one that was different from the one my parents lived. I did not believe that healthy marriages existed because the life I saw my parents live was not completely healthy. I avoided marriage like the plague because I did not want to be handed off to another man as a liability or responsibility. I wanted to be recognized and loved for the woman I was, and I wanted to join a marital union because of love, rather than being placed in an arranged marriage. The part of me that still craved to receive the right love also did not believe that men of Pakistani culture had the capacity within them to love unconditionally.

I always went against the tide and did things differently. Women like me are often seen as a threat to patriarchy in our culture. I was one of the first women in our family to gain a post-secondary education, the first to earn awards and scholarships, the first to build a successful career, the first to buy her own car, the first to marry late (at the age of twenty-seven), the first to live in Mecca, Saudi Arabia with her husband for nine months (which every single Muslim dreams of), and the first to separate from her husband following the birth of their daughter.

Women in our culture are encouraged to continue living in abusive marriages for the sake of their children, and so was I. For a long time, I did exactly as I was advised, but a part of me also knew that the ones who claimed to love me actually did not. Finally, I walked away from my abusive marriage because in searching and longing for answers and love, I nearly committed suicide. I knew deep within me that I would be happy if love existed in my marriage, but that was not the case. Oppressors and abusers surrounded me while I was living in a long-distance relationship with my husband, and that situation did not exude true love.

The pain in my chest and the pit in my stomach became deeper and darker. I had nowhere else to turn but inward and upward. I didn't feel like I belonged in this world, but my soul had unfinished work on planet Earth. So, I dragged my body along to search for my soul's purpose and for the love that happy and fulfilled people often talked about. I believed that if others talked about and embodied love, then it must exist. I just didn't know why I hadn't found true love yet.

Rising from abuse and rock-bottom has its glorious moments, in which you are left with only yourself and you get to become the one to lift yourself up. No one else can do for you what you can do for yourself. My journey inward led me to dig up the darkest corners of my heart and soul. In that process, the pain and trauma within me resurfaced. The pain and memories that led me to believe that true love did not exist needed a safe passage to be released. The part of me that felt unworthy of love needed to be shown how beautiful and worthy she actually was.

The lessons I learned in my journey toward myself are a lot more valuable than any lesson I learned during my formal education and a successful corporate career. These lessons have taught me that my broken-ness is the most beautiful side of me. My broken-ness is my human-ness, and every ounce of me is valuable and worthy of my own unconditional love. This is when I had the privilege of falling in love with every aspect of myself, which has been so incredibly empowering and liberating.

Dear Love,

I found you when I least expected it.
I found you in a place that I never
cared to look until I had no other option.
I found you and I am writing to you
to say that I love you.

I love you for never leaving me.
I am sorry that I took this long to
acknowledge your existence within me.

I see you now.
I see that you were always a part of me.
The love that I spent my entire life
seeking and searching outside of me
was always within me, just waiting
to be discovered.

Dear love,
Thank you for believing in me.

The moment I found love within me, the sharp pain in my chest began to fade, the pit in my stomach eased, and my mind, body, and soul began to heal in miraculous ways. I am sharing my lifelong struggle to find the true love which was within me all along, to remind you that the love you may also be searching for is within you. It always has been.

Look within, forgive yourself, and fall so incredibly and deeply in love with every aspect of you because loving the queen is a true privilege. And you, my love, are a *queen*.

Once you have recognized how amazing and worthy you are, the next step is to do the inner work to strengthen and reprogram your belief system. I often get asked by my clients how one falls in love with themselves, how to believe in self-worth, and how to forgive. I have a simple process I have used with myself and my clients to do just that.

This is my secret daily self-love routine, and I challenge you to follow it consistently the very first thing in the morning for the next thirty days to reprogram your mind. The intention of this routine is for you to pour unconditional love into yourself before you start your day. You must fill your own cup every single day before you pour into others.

Instructions:

1. Repeat the following statements ten to fifteen times each or for two to three minutes each while looking in the mirror straight into your own eyes with love and compassion.
2. Try your best to be present with yourself in the moment.

Affirmations:

1. I deeply and completely love, accept, and forgive myself.
2. [State your name], I love you. You are amazing!
3. Everything is always working out for me. I am safe and I am taken care of.
4. I give myself permission to receive the love, respect, loyalty, compassion, abundance, health, peace, and healing that I desire.
5. I give myself permission to release what no longer serves me.

My next challenge to you is to be extremely gentle with yourself. You must make it your mission to catch your negative thoughts and self-talk throughout the day. The moment you catch the negativity, you must pause right away and make a conscious effort to shift it into positive. If you have had your thoughts run on auto-pilot for years, then let this challenge push you to be a gentle observer of the negative stories you have been telling yourself in your mind in order to shift them into positive.

For the next thirty days, make yourself a priority. Put yourself on top of your to-do list, take yourself out on dates and treat yourself with the immense love, honor, and respect that you deserve from others. If you are not used to putting yourself first, then this challenge might lead you toward guilt, shame, or embarrassment. If it does, then right in that moment when you feel those emotions, I want you to recommit to yourself. You must tell yourself a different story. You must remind yourself of how incredibly worthy you are of your own love.

Abuse does not always come in the form of physical or sexual mistreatment; sometimes it can be subtle and self-inflicted. Not giving yourself permission to nurture yourself is a form of abuse. Not giving yourself permission to take care of your body or fuel it with the necessary nutrients every single day is a form of abuse. Running yourself depleted of positivity, self-love, honor, respect, care, and nurturing while treating yourself like you are worthless is a form of abuse. You need to be the one to break the cycle of abuse that you have put yourself through and allowed others to put you through.

Society has programmed women to view themselves with a sense of lack and unworthiness. The truth is, you are an incredibly powerful human being and you have every right to love and be loved unconditionally, but it all starts with you. If you need to scream positive statements at the top of your lungs every single day in order for the divine truth to settle within you, then do just that.

Only you know what you need to give yourself on a daily basis. A part of you also knows why you have not been able to receive the love you desire. This part of you has been hiding past pain, memories, and trauma. This is the little girl in you who is terrified and hurt. Self-love will lead you on the path of healing that little girl. She needs to be loved and nurtured by you and only you. She needs to forgive, and only you can lead her down the path of forgiveness. It all starts with self-love.

Forgiveness can be a daunting and painful thought, but it doesn't have to be. Forgiveness allows you to acknowledge your pain by giving yourself the space to not only articulate what happened but also to voice it within yourself. This process is extremely empowering because so many of us tend to hide and suppress our own pain from ourselves. In a way, we carry out the work of abusers and haters even after they are no longer a part of our lives.

I thought I had forgiven my father when he passed away in 2013. I was in Saudi Arabia during my first trimester when I received the news. It felt like a dream. I was heartbroken, but I prayed for him and forgave him that day for the years of pain

I had held onto. When my marriage fell apart two years later, I was advised by a spiritual healer that I needed to forgive my father further. I was told I had manifested this mess because the little girl in me needed to see him differently — this time with unconditional love and compassion.

Forgiveness was not easy. It took a lot out of me to forgive, and maybe a part of me still held on. Receiving the signed Islamic Divorce from my husband after living separately for five years helped me see my father through a different lens. I saw how he was the better man who had just buried himself under guilt and pain from his childhood. It was like a shift in perspective, a state that I had not been able to reach before regardless of how hard I tried. Forgiveness helps you change your perspective.

I am going to break down forgiveness into a few simple yet extremely effective steps for you to follow along with your self-love ritual. Forgiveness is a part of loving yourself again. It leads you back to yourself and your divine truth. It leads you toward self-love.

Instructions:

1. Make a list of all the people who have made you feel unworthy or caused you pain.
2. Make a list of every single painful memory related to every single person you listed.
3. Write a detailed forgiveness letter to each person, one by one.
4. Release each letter by either burning it and/or flushing it down the toilet.
5. Cut the energetic cord and release each of them with love.

Details:

1. Forgiveness Letter: In the process of writing this letter, I encourage you to be extremely detailed by listing all the pain each person caused you. Really dig deep and pull out all of those suppressed emotions you wish you could share with them if you ever had the chance. These could include anger, sadness, resentment, regret, guilt, shame, embarrassment, or blame. Allow yourself the space to voice it all and to feel all of the emotions that you need to release out of your body.

   Split the letter into the following sections:
   a. This is what you did to me.
   b. This is how it made me feel.
   c. This is how my life has been impacted as a result.
   d. This is how I wish things would have happened instead.
   e. Closing Statement: What you did to me is your karma, and it will come back to you in this life and the hereafter. You are free to go in your life, but not in my life and my world any longer. I now release you, along with all the pain and memories attached to you. I forgive you, I release you, I send you love, and I wish you well.

2. Releasing the letter: Repeat your closing statement while ripping up the letter, burning it, and/or flushing it down the toilet. Allow your tears and emotions to flow out of you throughout this process.

3. Cut the energetic cord: After the letter has been released and the emotions have been processed, sit down in a quiet spot and meditate. Visualize the person sitting in front of you. Imagine a cord connecting the two of you at the heart or any other area of the body where the emotions and pain were held. Visualize yourself cutting the cord while repeating your closing statement.

Throughout the forgiveness process, self-love, care, and nurturing are extremely important. You are releasing heavy and suppressed emotions. Let them go into their own world and release them from yours.

And know this . . .

You deserve better.
You deserve to be loved.
You deserve to be fulfilled.
You deserve to be more intentional
with your desires.

Do not cheat yourself
out of your own happiness.
Only you can give yourself
all that you and your soul
have been aching for.

And it all starts with loving yourself
every single day.

I DEEPLY AND COMPLETELY LOVE,
ACCEPT, AND FORGIVE MYSELF.
I AM LOVE AND
THAT IS MY TRUEST TRUTH.

CHAPTER 10

Lost Identity in the Wrong Love

"Being authentic takes fearless confidence in who you are. You must believe you are enough."

By: Habiba Jessica Zaman

Habiba Jessica Zaman

www.habibazaman.com

ig: @habibti_zaman I fb: @habibajessicazaman I fb: @northstarofgeorgia

· · · · · · · · · · · ·

HABIBA JESSICA ZAMAN, NCC LPC, Has a master's degree in professional counseling specializing in trauma and is owner of North Star of Georgia Counseling. With fifteen years of experience in the counseling field including counseling, advocacy, guidance, and education, she believes that as awareness of one's fears, perceptions, desires, and strengths increases, one can make successful life changes. The development of self-awareness by becoming more honest with oneself can initiate the authenticity that often results in healing, transformation, and a fuller life. Habiba has thirteen publications that started with *But I'm Just Playing*, a children's book published in 2012. Her latest co-authored works, *Beautifully Bare, Undeniably You,* and the original *You've Got This, Mama,* both released in 2018. She also coauthored in the previous volume of this series, *Dear Time, Are You on My Side?* Habiba is of Bangladeshi and American descent. She has two children and lives in Atlanta, Georgia with her family.

---

*"The most painful thing is losing yourself
in the process of loving someone too much,
and forgetting that you are special too."*
~ Ernest Hemingway

I CAN'T. I'M FED UP. That's all I have to say about it. I am beyond over-whelmed. I am flooded with emotion. My hands are shaking and I can't swallow the lump in my throat that feels like a piece of jagged metal because I am using all my power to keep myself from letting that tear fall. Just that one teardrop will melt whatever glue that's holding me together. I can't let it happen. I can't crack. Because it won't be a crack. It won't be catharsis or cleansing. Allowing this tear to escape would mean the unraveling of my carefully sewn-together tapestry of the bullshit mask I've been showing to the world. This mask that may never slip, not even for a moment. The constant need to be strong and collected and put-together. The engine that keeps this interlocking universe of mine functioning. It will all just crumble. It's just too much.

I give, and I give, and I give. I give cheerfully. I am a helper and nurturer by nature, so I do it. I do it because I love you and because I want to show you matter to me. And it still feels as though it is not enough. I am under scrutiny for all my effort, and it seems like that judgement is still there no matter what I do. I am too this or too that. I am too tired after work and I don't make you a priority even though I give every waking moment that I have to spare to you. I used to love to dance: Latin, ballroom, Bollywood, belly dancing, you name it. Now, the only opportunity I have to dance is when I am waltzing around the house with my cat to the most recent John Legend or Ed Sheer-an song. Or painting . . . when was the last time I picked up a paintbrush? Music? I used to play the cello, and it brought me so much peace; its warm, dark, powerful sound would transcend space and time and take me to a place deep within where I felt the passion of the music reverberate through my being.

Where did that person go? Where is the woman who used to get lost in the imaginary realm of the next novel or story, who felt one with the music, who advocated and fought for everyone, whether it was a child who needed to be stood up for or the woman who needed to be taken to the shelter? Where is the woman who would dance in the summer storm regardless of the dress and satin heels as she ran to the car? When was the last time I was one with her? I am giving my all to this other person and to my children. Every breath I take serves to show them I love them and that they matter. Somehow, all they see is this version of me that doesn't exist.

I am not who you are defining me to be. Somehow, I have become the catalyst of all your suffering. Even though you said you would be here at a certain time and came forty minutes late without a call or text, I am the one who is too stern and too calculated. I take things too seriously and expect too much. Even though you chose to take a seven- and nine-year-old to a movie that exposed them to violence and brief nudity, I am the one who neurotically made a big deal out of nothing when the kids had nightmares. Even though it is your assumptions that created the chaos of misunderstanding in your mind, it is my tone that makes you too anxious to ask to clarify. I am too cold, I am too angry, I am too much of everything.

To show that I am not these things, I temper myself. I don't go to dance classes alone because you will feel left out if you stay home to watch the kids. Then I decide it's better not to go to these classes at all because you do not pick up the steps as I do, and that makes you feel inept. I make sure I call you as soon as I leave the office so you do not feel as though I am talking to someone else. I stay awake and watch another episode with you, even though I am bone-tired, so you feel like I am spending time with you. I anticipate every possible outcome so that the kids will always be cared for, and so I don't show I am angry or upset when something else is neglected. Because if I show anger or frustration, I am this heartless, judgmental, explosive monster who makes you feel unsafe. Even though I didn't raise my voice, and even if it wasn't heard in my voice, my face showed it and my expression hurts you. I've learned to temper myself. It's not worth the guilt, the struggle, the conflict. Nothing much has changed as I go day by day, but when I look back I see how much of myself I have left behind in an attempt to tone down what makes me, me. The passion, the joy, the drive, the dancer, the musician, the artist, the playfulness, the fighter. I abandoned myself, I gave up my passions, I forgot about my dreams, and I lost my identity in loving you. The fire that once burned so brilliantly has dimmed down so much that I don't know if even the ember will glow. I am now left as a shell without a soul.

♥ ♥ ♥

It is a very precious and rare thing to find love. Love is enchanting, and nothing can compare to the experience. We long for love, crave it, and feel the loss of it as if we were going through a physical withdrawal. It is a universal yearning — to find someone who will finally see us, accept us, and fill our lives with vibrant color. To open and expose ourselves to someone, to love them and hope to be loved in return is by far one of the most vulnerable things we can do as humans. Somehow, the search to find love has been overshadowed by the need to find "the one."

This concept of finding your better half has become the most damaging construct in our society. We teach both men and women that we are not whole on our own, that this life is not beautiful and worth experiencing unless we have that special someone to share it with. That the key to our happiness lies in someone else's pocket. This construct starts in childhood, when messages of being alone equate to loneliness in our psyches. We are taught that someone eating alone must not have anyone to share their meal with or that a person who travels the globe alone must be solitary by force. How limiting it is to believe that loneliness is felt only in the absence of people, when many of us know intimately that we can be surrounded by people and still feel intensely alone. We must never allow our happiness to depend on a relationship. As Becca Lee so poignantly articulated, [t]he surest way to lose your self-worth is by trying to find it through the eyes of others.

The most damaging belief we can hold is that we must give our all in a relationship, that to love means to sacrifice everything for that love, to be selfless and put the other above ourselves. That is not love; that is dependence. Think about when you first fell for each other: the connection was created and solidified as you each revealed more about yourselves, through the shared laughs, the moments when you admired them for their triumphs, the attraction and fondness that grew as you found similarities and shared new experiences. Two distinct expressions of authentic lives spun the enchantment. *That* is the beginning of love. You each have your core values, interests, social support groups, your most unique identity that made you desirable when the relationship began. What happened?

For most of us, the idea of love equals sacrifice from our first experience with it: our parents. We seek approval by partaking in behaviors to prove that we are good children; seeking that sense of validation and worth often leads to over-giving because if we give more, then they will love us back more.

What we need to strive for in our romantic relationships instead is a partnership. Partnership requires compromise, *not* sacrifice. What is the difference? In sacrifice, both parties miss out on something. Through compromise, both have their needs, based on their core values, met. In a partnership, there is no feeling of being forced. There are no "I have to" moments or fears of consequence in a true partnership. Both partners commit to respecting each other's values and boundaries. There's true understanding of what makes the other person feel loved and appreciated in the knowledge about which lines are not acceptable to cross. Partners take the time to meet the other person with a sense of curiosity and practice, finding new aspects of one another to learn from and to nurture. It is difficult to take another person for granted when you see them as a being who is always growing and always evolving. Partnerships allow the freedom to explore and to grow together. Dependent relationships require things to stay the same.

How can we form meaningful partnerships? Authenticity.

Being authentic takes fearless confidence in who you are. You must believe you are enough. You also must know that it isn't a reflection of your worth if your partner doesn't understand this: it's not about you. Rather, it means the intricacies of what makes you uniquely yourself just aren't a good match with them, or they have failed to see how rare your love is. It is not for us to prove our value to others. We do not need to try to convince someone that we are enough. The right people will feel it and work to keep you.

Our relationship with ourselves forms the foundation of all the other relationships we cultivate. Therefore, our relationship with ourselves is the relationship we need to nurture and prioritize so we can attract people who reflect what we are looking for in interpersonal connections. Otherwise, we will continue to sacrifice at the expense of ourselves and ultimately look back only to realize that we have become only a shell of who we once were. Our respect and love for ourselves help us set strong boundaries, live our values, and find the courage to walk away from any relationship that doesn't encourage us to be the best version of ourselves.

Wouldn't it be wonderfully simple if I told you that all you need to do is become vulnerable, ask for what you need, and share your truth? That is in fact the recipe, yet few people can articulate their truth or their needs when asked.

There are several factors to identify when embarking on the journey to understand how you came to be uniquely you, which I discuss in depth in my other book, *Beautifully Bare, Undeniably You*:

1. What events influenced the way you see the world.
2. How you think, positively or negatively.
3. How you react to events and experiences.
4. Who you are and why you are that way.

In order to articulate your wants and needs both to potential partners and to those closest to you with whom you already share your heart, you must know your identity and be secure in it. Here are a few questions to ask to get you started on that journey. What are your passions? What makes you feel alive? What situations bring you bursts of positive energy that are not attached to other people? What are some ideals for which you would fight? What are some of your non-negotiables, or what I love to call your "fuck no" boundaries?

Confidence in your worth comes with a secure identity, which will help you ask confidently for what you need and politely decline situations that are not in alignment with your core identity. Think of your identity as a handbook to all things *you*. Handbooks provide guidelines for what is acceptable in an environment or a relationship and for the expected consequences of neglecting or violating those guidelines of acceptability.

Reflect on your current relationships. What are the consequences, if any, when your boundaries are violated? What steps do you take to ensure that you will not accept a particular treatment? What do your loved ones have to do to get back into your good graces, and do they end up just repeating the behavior a few weeks or months later? To keep the peace, how much of what's important to you are you willing to gloss over, dismiss, or ignore? Why does keeping that peace take precedence over upholding your core values?

Each time you are reluctant to stand up for what you believe in, your subconscious takes a hit on your self-esteem and self-worth. Of course, we can rationalize consciously that we are choosing our battles, but the subconscious doesn't work the way our conscious brain does. It takes things at face value — this is just one more time you are not standing up for yourself. When you avoid *this* battle or *that* comment, you take a step away from yourself until one day you look back and see just how much things have changed, recognizing that the reflection in the mirror no longer matches your truth.

The only sure way to prevent this from happening is to be sure of where you stand, how you want to feel, and how you want to be treated in your relationships. Be strong in your values and set powerful boundaries to protect your time and energy. Own and speak your truth. Nurture your unique identity and cultivate your independence. Remember that the ultimate approval comes from you. Your identity exists separately from any relationship, so choose friendships and relationships that add value to your life and are in alignment with who you want to be. Listen to your own intuition and trust that it will steer you toward what is important.

After all that I have lost — my voice, my security, my identity — it is very difficult to look for hope. You meet someone, connect on an intimate level, and the excitement starts to bubble to the surface. It makes you feel alive and feel seen and believe that perhaps, just perhaps, this time they will accept, cherish, and value you for *you*. I've had those moments, and though they did not last, they have helped me learn more about who I am.

I may not know what love is, but I most certainly know what love is not. I have learned that if at any point I shield, sequester, or alter any aspect of what I need from the person I am with, it is not going to work. I am not to shrink to fit into their mold. My needs come from my values, and those values are the building blocks of the foundation of my identity. In order to love me, a potential partner must acknowledge and accept these components of me. If not, my resentment will build from the relentless feeling of being misunderstood and unaccepted, and it will tear us apart.

Here is what I have deduced so far: I am looking for an openness to build a long-term partnership, even while understanding we can't guarantee that's where it will end up. I am looking for stability and security in that commitment. I want to know what I can reasonably anticipate from my partner with respect to contact, emotional and physical intimacy, reliability, connection, safety, and security, but I acknowledge that these things look different to different people, and that assumptions and expectations will ruin a relationship. That's where the conversation needs to take place. It is no longer about sacrificing myself to make things work; it is about owning and accepting where I stand and finding a partner who can stand with me effortlessly. I know they are out there somewhere, making their way to me.

Every relationship is a give-and-take. We give love, encouragement, comfort, safety, shared experiences, laughter, support, guidance, and passion. Doesn't it make sense that we should be able to expect the same in return? You matter, so you need to make yourself a priority. Saying yes to you does not make you selfish, nor does it make someone else less worthy. If you are saying yes to someone else and saying no to yourself as a result, you are automatically saying that their needs are superior to yours. It is never okay to meet the needs of someone else at the *expense* of your own. In a true partnership, coexistence does not come at the expense of either person — rather, both person's needs are met, even if it is not at the same time.

Remember, no one else ever could ever offer what you have to offer the way you offer it, with your essence. There is no comparison, so learn your truth, figure out what makes you uniquely you, and own it. Share your most authentic self with the world, and you will find that those who speak your language will gravitate to you, and stay.

I APPROACH ALL
THINGS WITH LOVE.

CHAPTER 11

Chasing Light

*"Allow the self-discovery process to be
the open doorway to self-love."*

By: J.R. Huff

J.R. Huff

JENNIFER HUFF KNOWS NO LIMITATIONS. A free-spirited, intuitive, nature-loving, fire-walking badass, she recently discovered her passion for teaching holistic self-care. She is a living example of the healing power of love. Her spiritual, mental, and physical philosophies were forged in her own experiences in sorrow, self-discovery, and truest joy. Her diverse and expansive studies provide her with knowledge of self-healing, esoteric and occult sciences, holistic psychology, archeology, and Stephen King. She is fully committed to exposing every human possible to their own capacities of healing and co-creation, encouraging others to fully embrace the chaos of the universe, love themselves completely, and break cycles of self-sabotage. She gratefully acknowledges the love and support of her husband, the Magnificent Hippie in Oregon, and dedicates her work to her son Kayun, whom she loves the most.

BY A MERE TWENTY-FIVE YEARS OF AGE, I found myself.

Most often, I found myself curled in a fetal position on the floor, alone and crying. And I don't mean beautiful tears that drip daintily from soft, soulful eyes. I mean an ugly cry: snot pouring, head pounding, body aching.

We are borne from madness.

How else to describe the state of being we find ourselves in, but utter chaos?

In the grips of this insanity, we close our eyes and sink. Our perception of the outside reality reflects the uncertainty we feel in ourselves, and often it is horrible to look at. Out of self-defense, we shut our eyes to it and emphatically reject it. To protect ourselves from any further damage, we withdraw as if the only place we will truly find peace is inside ourselves.

During any routine day, before my epiphany on the bathroom floor, I would care for my young son and try to earn a living. I would send him to school, pray for the best, and struggle to support us with minimum wage and hope. The juggling act of single parenthood kept me incredibly busy most hours of most days. In the few moments I would achieve actual solitude, the only thing I was physically capable of was getting comfortable with a bottle of whiskey and crying uncontrollably.

In the moments when I was haunted by trauma and past abuse, time became irrelevant. All that existed was pain. I could fill the majority of my time with the mundane, but the pain would resurface the second that my attention was diverted. Memories would flood my thoughts, and my body would be obligated to release that flood. Sometimes it poured out while I was standing in line at the grocery store. Once, the dam broke in my son's school as I sat waiting in the pick-up line.

By the time I reached twenty-five, I was struggling with a diagnosis of schizophrenia, regular panic attacks, bouts of narcissistic rage, and depression episodes that lasted months. A single parent and an orphan by choice, I rocked myself like a crying child on that cold bathroom floor, wrapping myself in a cocoon of safe darkness. Closing my eyes to the ugliness of my world. As far as I knew, "normal" was a relative term: my reality alternated between surviving trauma and loathing myself. Love was a myth, life was a chaotic struggle, and peace was reserved for holy men.

"The wound is where the light enters."

~ Rumi

The breaking point is required.

The part of me I wanted my son to experience — a loving mom — was the part of me I eventually learned to create. By the standards of the narrative that had been *given* to me, I would never be able to parent without violence and rage. Because of my disease, I would always have uncontrollable mood swings. I could never sustain a loving relationship. I was broken mentally, emotionally, and spiritually. *If* the Loving Mother existed within me, I could never predict when she would appear. I knew I wouldn't be able to keep her around if she ever popped up. And this erratic, often violent, existence would be the "normal" of the rest of my life.

The part of me that spoke the loudest, the truest voice of my soul, screamed in outrage. She wept. My heart shattered completely at the prospect of a life devoid of love. *Go ahead and run every potential relationship right out the door, right now, and accept that no other human could love such a person. How could they?* I damn sure didn't love me.

As I lay there on the bathroom floor, rubbing endless amounts of snot off my unlovable face, I decided I wanted something different. I agreed with my soul and cried out in unison with her. I wanted to change, to flip the script, to alter the narrative of my life. Was I crazy, or capable of protecting my son like a wild animal? Was I broken, or just a mess that could be cleaned? After all, I reasoned, how could people who had spent such limited time with me really know more about me than I could know about myself? Simply put — they couldn't. I was the only person with me 24/7, and I had proven myself capable of surviving that way. It was time to re-learn all of the things about me. Against all odds, I attempted to control the chaos with which I had become so disgustingly familiar.

Analyzing the scene with 20/20 hindsight reveals the scattered nature of self-love: the non-linear process of self-questioning, extensive searching for answers, and discovering new questions. The sometimes uncomfortable experiences of libraries and internet searches, intense conversations with therapists and doctors that lead to summiting mountains of research papers. The exploration of words and phrases requiring their own dictionaries, combining esoteric study and religious skepticism to forge a kind of spiritual reckoning through conscious awakening. For me, self-love was a combination of beliefs, educated guesses, and therapeutic diagnoses. Sometimes it was no conversation at all, just days of empty silence filled with echoing thoughts. I sought out any and all perspectives on the human mind, body, and soul. *Yoga for wellness? How does that work? Food can affect your mood? Prove it. Not all science is perfect? Show me.* I learned that my level of awareness on such matters was both woeful and full of potential. I educated myself. I evaluated the overwhelming amount of information for over ten years.

I learned more about myself in that decade alone than I could ever fit in a single book. I was teaching myself about myself to control myself. In this search-and-research style of self-education, I began to do something rebellious, something utterly insane: I began to change. This excited my inner bitch in ways I can't describe. I discovered whole, unbroken parts of myself. Entire facets that were not just lovable, they were *desirable.*

As I sorted through the mess of *me,* searching for worth and salvageability, I revealed a truth. The light that now poured freely into my once comfortably dark cocoon exposed the unknown. There were indeed unlovable pieces — bitterness, sadness, regret, and even hate. But that glittering light revealed the possibilities — joy, kindness, passion, and especially, love. As I analyzed and scrutinized, I gave myself permission to be honest. All of that chaos, that beautiful mess, was presenting me an opportunity. Shifting my perspective shifted my reality.

I perceived my anger as a survival tool: my defense system. I saw where my struggle to survive was actually my Warrior at work. I was alive, so therefore my archetypal Warrior was victorious. I had a heart full of love for my child, which meant the Loving Mother existed. My mistakes were my Sinner, my desire for change was my Saint. My anger was justified — I had every right to be angry with people who had shed my blood. This meant I knew justice, and the lack of it. I could be fair. There was so much more to me than rage and depression — I'm a plethora of personalities!

The one question that can open the door to actual enlightenment began to surface from the desperate depths: "What if?"

Like the divine nature of chaotic destruction, the metamorphosis is sacred. What if there is more? Only the caterpillar intuitively knows. After all, the caterpillar is not born with wings. But it *is* born with everything needed to become the butterfly.

> *"Give a woman pain and she will turn it into power; give that woman chaos, and she'll create peace."*
> ~ R.H. Sin

The process of detoxification is an unstable one. The body becomes attuned to whatever state of being the mind has been dwelling in. In the state of discontent, we become uncomfortable. In the state of fear, we become flooded with instinctual response. By habit and subconscious influence, we become accustomed to toxicity when it runs rampant. Learning to remove all the toxicity was one of the most difficult challenges I've ever faced. Starting small, I removed every piece of paper with my name on it that contained descriptions of me I refused to accept. If it had a "never," "incapable," "can't," or a similar word creating a written limitation, I tossed it out. I got rid of whole books.

I then expanded this release of toxic language to human beings. Removing people from your life can be a harder challenge but it is one with the greatest reward. Cutting certain people out frees you from their opinions of your life. This gives back the power to you, its rightful owner. This process helps you prove to yourself that your own opinion of your life matters the most.

As I became more effective at detoxification, it evolved. I stopped depending on alcohol and drugs to provide an escape, and I started hiking and traveling. Every time I removed something or someone, I replaced it with a healthier option. The more I worked to replace the bad feelings I had for myself, the better I felt.

I set in place the firm and concrete belief that better for me meant better for my son. Communication pathways opened themselves between me and my son, and likewise between me and the man who became my husband. The love in our relationships grew and expanded in harmony with the gratitude I began to feel for the changes in my life. It got easier to use my words to express my stress, fears, and challenges. Violence became something I could choose to resort to, or choose to reject.

The greatest accomplishment in learning to love myself has been in allowing change to happen. In the same way I allowed myself to shrink and weep, the way I permitted my tears to build my cocoon, I accepted that damage had been done. I allowed myself to hurt from it. I allowed myself to ask the "what if" question about my potential to heal and grow. I let curiosity bring out the best in me.

I allowed myself to receive the love that poured freely from my son, husband, and supporters. I didn't fight the days I stayed in bed to sleep, cry, and recuperate. I agreed to rising early just for the sunrise and the silence.

If I need to be the loving and nurturing mother, I am her. If I need to be the one who laughs instead of cries, I let myself laugh like a fool. If I need to say "no" after countless times of saying "yes," then so be it. If the creative urge to make something strikes . . . get it? I don't have to look, sound, think, act, or live in any *one* particular way. I can be many, and I can be none. I have given myself the ultimate permission to change as often or as little as I see fit. With this authority granted, I love myself with full acceptance.

Perhaps even more important than allowing the changes comes the requirement of patience. I invested the single most valuable resource into myself: time. I did not force myself to become fixed or healed from my traumas within a certain time frame. Yes, I set goals, and I achieved them with reasonable swiftness. But the standard was set for me, by me.

As a woman, I had several social expectations already set in place before I was born. I would be a daughter, born to a mother and father. I would be a sister, grouped with my siblings. I would be a schizophrenic, following a long line of women in my bloodline. All of those predetermined classifications were just waiting for me.

Staring myself in the eyes in the bathroom mirror, warm water still dripping from my puffy face, I asked, "What if you wiped that clean, and started from the beginning again? What if, just for shits and giggles, you changed?" Obviously, not *all* of it can wash off in a single moment of clarity. But a clean surface is nonetheless a perfect start. At worst, I could prove them all right and be miserable the rest of my life. At best, I could surprise everyone (myself included) and beat the odds. I gently patted my face dry, found my son running around in the yard, and hugged him with every ounce of love I could feel.

I used to think the light at the end of the tunnel was a thing that was to be constantly chased, but never caught; that the overwhelming accuracy of the tunnel analogy was the saddest truth of human existence. One would always work toward that elusive light and would only exit the tunnel at the end of their natural life. Now I see things differently. You can decide to let the light come to you.

It isn't a tunnel. It's a cocoon. The darkness isn't permanent. It is a powerful tool for metamorphosis. The light is proof you have changed. The moment you step into it, embracing the changes that have caused disproportionate amounts of loss and gain, is the moment you unfold your wings. The existence of unimaginable beauty awaits you, if you but leap into its blinding brightness. Your previous existence as a caterpillar will make sense once you've experienced the heartfelt flight of self-acceptance.

The harsh truth is not everyone knows that love doesn't have to hurt. The freedom in that same truth is discovered in your capacity to choose to love yourself, in the ways you haven't been loved by others, in the ways that only you can, and that is your superpower as a human: your ability to choose. One of the greatest joys of life is the variety of choice it provides. Changes are inevitable for caterpillar and human alike — the acceptance of this fact is the transition from cocoon to flight, from darkness to light. You can unleash your ability to choose to redefine the chaos and utilize its potential. Choose to see yourself in that new light. Discover yourself and be impressed by your potential. Make dedicated choices to understand all of the things about yourself from your zodiac sign to your blood type, eating habits, and sleep patterns. Learn from your repetitive behavioral cycles that expose the parts of your soul calling for your attention. Explore your speech patterns that express your emotions, and more. You will undoubtedly see parts of yourself that you want to change. Start with where you are and what you have. Take your time. Allow the self-discovery process to be the open doorway to self-love. In the breaking, you will discover the most beautiful truth: there is more.

♥ ♥ ♥

Here is reading material that helped shift and expand my perspective of myself:

- de Laszlo, V.S. (editor). (1993). *The Basic Writings of C.G. Jung*. New York, NY: Modern Library.

- Feuerstein, G. (2003). *The Deeper Dimensions of Yoga: Theory and Practice*. Boulder, CO: Shambhala Publications.

- Singer, M. A. (2007). *The Untethered Soul*. Oakland, CA: New Harbinger Publications.

SECTION 2

READY TO LOVE ANOTHER

LOVE WINS.

CHAPTER 12

Love Is My Superpower

"Never underestimate the alchemizing resiliency of a heart that chooses love."

BY: DANIELLE LAURA

Danielle Laura

www.danielle-laura.com

ig: @_daniellelaura_ I fb: @daniellelauracoaching

. . . .

DANIELLE IS A mission-driven former corporate medical executive turned spiritual entrepreneur who has spent the last decade innovating therapy work and leading teams of change makers. This work has given her an exceptional understanding of human behavior and what it takes for lasting transformation and success at every level. As the founder of H.O.T. Souls™ Individual and Couples Coaching, Danielle is passionate about helping people shift their entire paradigm so they can shift and change the world through deep honesty, openness, and transparency. Her mission is to help change makers ground into their truth, master their gifting to amplify their zone of genius, cultivate H.O.T., thriving relationships, and up-level their life in transformative ways in order to live fully expressed lives professionally and personally while making their greatest impact. Danielle has a master's degree in counseling, a bachelor's degree in health science, and is a Certified Reiki Master Healer.

I DRANK THE TOXIC POISON OF ANOTHER, whose drug of choice was never going to be me. Isn't it crazy how we can lose ourselves trying to save someone else? As empathic, heart-centered women with healing gifts, we can sometimes find ourselves in cycles of over-giving, over-extending, and over-sacrificing in service to others, because we think our love alone can heal their wounds. We want to help everyone around us and leave them better off than before they knew us, but before we know it, we are trapped in the vicious cycle of losing our connection with our selves and forgetting how powerful, beautiful, and magnificent we truly are. We unknowingly give our power away as our worth becomes defined by others. It's an odd situation when we want to help another heal their wounds, even at the cost of destroying our own heart. However, the real magic happens when we can turn our perceived greatest weakness into our favorite superpower.

"Until death do you part." In marriage vows, this phrase refers to a physical death, but what about the part of your spirit that dies every day from the toxic schemes of the person who is supposed to love you unconditionally? I wanted to be married only once; divorce was not an option for me. Growing up with a strong Christian background, I took the covenant of marriage very seriously, and I meant every word of the vows I wrote. Little did I know at the time that the vows spoken by the man I married were intertwined with calculated lies, hidden agendas, and inner demons that were soon about to enter my world.

Addiction was the very scary circumstance that slowly altered my perception of reality. His mind was so warped and overtaken by sexual addictions that he couldn't see the fullness of beauty that I embodied, or really any aspect of me. His mind and heart were elsewhere, living in the daily delusion of justification and lies. "You're just okay looking" was one of the many things he told me. I don't think I will ever forget that moment, just a few weeks into marriage, when everything stood still as his precarious brown eyes penetrated straight into mine, breaking my soul.

The following days, months, and years only got worse. I suffered in silence to uphold his reputation and not cause drama or gossip in our small southern town. A shift began to take place within my psyche as he continued to show total disregard for me by spending all of his time elsewhere, by his actions and words not lining up, and by making comments like, "You could have more toned legs," or "You don't even look like you work out," or "Is eating that going to help you have more defined abs?" I slowly morphed from a confident, powerhouse woman who owned her worth and would never settle to an insecure girl who felt like she was just never going to be good enough. Despite being the woman who said she'd never change herself for a man, I began to do whatever I thought would make myself more appealing in his eyes and capture his heart once and for all. Isn't it crazy how our hearts have a mind of their own? I worked out six days a week instead of four, I cut all my hair off to suit his preference, I went above and beyond in supporting him in his work and affirming him. I even contemplated getting surgery to completely alter my body to his liking so that I could be his dream girl, in hopes that we could finally have a marriage that was as beautiful as our wedding.

Anxiety became my new state of consciousness. Standing in front of the mirror in my bra and panties, trying to grab hold of the nonexistent fat on my one-hundred-and-twelve-pound body, wearing constant feelings of disgust and unworthiness, I didn't recognize myself anymore. I was run down fighting the never-ending cycle of exhaustion and trying to silence my intuition every time it told me he was being unfaithful. I would fall asleep at night crying out to God as I prayed so fiercely over my husband for freedom, and I would start all over again the next morning, going through my days in constant prayer over his life and over our marriage.

I soon learned my intuition was right: he had been unfaithful for our entire marriage and had been carefully crafting stories to cover the lies he told while looking into my eyes became his *modus operandi*. As I retreated inward, I came to the realization that love does not mean giving up who you are. We have a choice: we can allow someone else to choose our life for us, or we can choose our life for ourselves and in turn take back our power and self-worth.

He may have never chosen me, but I understood that I had the power to choose myself, and that I am chosen by God. What I didn't realize at the time was that he was fighting a battle that had nothing to do with me. He was waging a war against himself, and nothing I did or didn't do would change that. We can pray all night until we fall asleep or go above and beyond to be what someone needs, but if they don't want to help themselves or see the real issue at hand, our love alone cannot save them.

I came to understand that my feelings of betrayal, trauma, bitterness, anger, and resentment were going to overtake my life if I didn't act quickly. There I sat one night on my bathroom floor, with three-day-old dirty hair, tear-soaked cheeks, and mascara stains falling onto the brim of my shirt, hugging the toilet bowl seat, sick from the anxiety overtaking my physical body, and it was in that moment I decided *I'm choosing to rise above.* I looked up to God and said, "I choose love." I decided in that moment that no matter what could happen, I was choosing to live in a vibrational state of love: heart-centered, pure, grace-filled, overflowing love.

That day, I committed to the journey of loving myself again and choosing to dissolve the lies spoken to destroy me — the lies of not being good enough, pretty enough, fit enough, successful enough, and all the other *not-enoughs*. In the depths of my soul, I already knew that I truly was more than enough. I knew that every ounce of love I craved was already inside of my heart, and it was just a matter of rediscovering it, bringing it to the surface, and defining a new path.

As we decided to get a divorce, I set out on my journey of healing, returning to a place of deep inner love within my heart, a self-love so grounded in the core truths of who God created me to be that my faith would become unshakable. I chose to live in a vibrational state of love, to work through my shadow, to extend grace no matter what, to be purposefully whole from within, and to live with peace in my heart. I made love my superpower.

Forgiveness was the first step on my journey to healing from heartbreak, and truly the catalyst to setting my soul free. Choosing to forgive yourself and the person who hurt you is one of the most emotionally difficult things to do, but its rewards for your soul are priceless. Forgiveness does not mean that you condone what the person did to you, and it does not mean that you have to welcome them back into your life again.

Releasing the negative energy of unforgiveness welcomes an unexplainable freedom, a newfound joy, and an indescribable peace. A beautiful exercise to help with this is to write a letter, first to yourself and then to the person who wronged you. Write out every bit of emotion that comes up for you without holding back. Allow yourself to go through the grieving process. As you write, you may feel a roller coaster of emotions — welcome and release them all. You may choose to not actually send the letter to the person who hurt you, and that's perfectly okay; use your judgment. The exercise itself will bring massive healing.

Choosing to get out of the pit of unforgiving also takes what I like to call getting H.O.T.: honest, open, and transparent with yourself. In order to create a new paradigm, we have to be raw and real with what we predominantly need and desire. Ask yourself the following questions and even journal it out to be completely clear-minded. What do you actually need and want in your life in order to thrive mentally, emotionally, spiritually, physically? This is the time to revisit and revamp, to focus on you and being the best version of you possible. What would the 2.0 version of you be doing? How would she be honoring herself? What decisions would she be making for her highest good? Free yourself: anything that no longer serves your highest good and that keeps you stuck in old patterns of self-deprecation or self-sabotage — now is the time to eliminate them from your life.

It's important to also make gratitude a daily practice. Consciously realizing how blessed you are, how you're divinely supported always, refuels your hope and brings joy to your heart. It's helpful to do this right when you wake up before you even get out of bed in order to become grounded, centered, and thankful as you start your day. It's amazing how your perspective shifts and how you allow yourself to receive goodness each day when you're in a vibration of gratitude. To take it a step further, keep a journal by your bed and write at least three things you're grateful for each day. On my hardest days, when I was working through the anger, this exercise took me out of the moment of living in past hurt and reminded me how blessed I truly was in my present reality.

Next, fall in love with ordinary moments by becoming powerfully present: the color of the leaves changing with the season, the taste of your favorite beverage as it hits your lips, the smile of a child looking up at you, the thrill of a good book, the freedom in your heart as you write to release your emotion, the beauty of a sunset, the quirky personality of your sweet dogs, a deep belly laugh with your friend over something hilarious, or the joy of a regular day knowing that you are divinely supported and always have more than enough. A large aspect of my inner healing was allowing my soul to be lit up by seemingly ordinary, everyday moments.

Sometimes an ordinary moment can bring up a lot of past emotion: extend yourself grace in those times, because in order to heal, you must feel. Give yourself permission to feel whatever feelings come to you instead of distracting, suppressing, or replacing those emotions with a more pleasant reality. In addition, don't label what comes up for you as good or bad. They just are, and they are part of your healing. Feel the emotion and release it accordingly. Cry if you need to cry. If you need to laugh uncontrollably, do it. If you feel the desire to dance or to punch a pillow or to sing out loud, don't hold back. This release creates an energy shift within the mind-body-soul connection that helps facilitate healing.

Also, don't sweat the small stuff. Be good to yourself, be fiercely loyal to your own healing journey, and give yourself all the love you need. Ask yourself what healing looks like for you. Does healing mean having a bath, meditating, getting your nails done, journaling, walking in nature, counseling? If you're laboring over something, ask yourself if this will matter five years from now. If the answer is "no," let it go.

Be the own love of your life and date yourself! Take yourself on solo dates to discover yourself again and realize you don't need someone to do everything with. Remind yourself how much you love your own company, and embrace the truth that you are more than enough. Buy yourself the flowers, take yourself to your favorite restaurant or to the new movie, splurge on yourself because you're worth it. Explore passions and hobbies you couldn't or didn't have time to do before. Do one thing every single day that brings you insurmountable joy. One thing I asked myself on a daily basis was, "What would bring me the most joy today?" Then I gave myself permission to do it, guilt-free. I can't promise you that making yourself a priority in this way will be easy — it wasn't a natural process for me. But I can tell you it was a catalyst to reminding me of what I deserve, aiding me in the process of becoming purposefully whole within my soul and regaining my inner power and sense of self-worth.

Another beautiful aspect of the healing journey after heartbreak is reconnecting with your sisterhood. Invest in your girlfriends again. Revive those connections with your soul sisters and family. Your inner circle will understand you and love you fiercely, while mirroring back to you all the ways you are incredible, beautiful, and worthy. Lean on your support system, and don't be afraid to ask for help on your weakest days. If you feel like you've lost your support system or friendships over the course of your relationship, I encourage you to take a step out of your comfort zone and join some organization where you can meet like minded individuals. Whether this is a workout class, an event for something you're passionate about, a service opportunity, or even an establishment you may not have explored before, extend yourself. Be open to receiving the love you've always deserved because there are many people who will mirror it back to you if you let them in.

As you continue to choose love and heal your heart, know that you always have the power to turn your mess into your message. When you're feeling brave and strong, start speaking your truth and sharing your story. Some of the deepest bonds I have in my life today are with people I opened up to by sharing my trials and my triumphs. Your experiences are your potent medicine to the world, and you never know who needs that medicine. I also encourage you to give of yourself to others — service is a beautiful way of healing. Volunteer your time and allow the joy of giving to fill your own soul back up. You may be surprised how many lives you can touch by the love that radiates through your presence — the presence of a soul whose superpower is love.

Being on the other side of my heartbreak now, and having returned to a place of deep inner love, respect, and resiliency, I can genuinely say that it's often the most heart-wrenching circumstances of our life that show us our most heart-centered mission. These missions have ripple effects into lives we may never even know about. Life is powerful when you are at peace in your own soul, and I believe self-love is the catalyst to any love worth accepting. Although my healing was at times both messy and glorious, I finally feel free, truly free, for the first time in my life because I chose to live in a vibrational state of love and to prioritize my soul's growth and healing. It's as though the scales have been taken off of my eyes and I can finally see clearly: because I am so fiercely grounded in my truth I can look at myself in the mirror and be in awe of my beauty, seeing how full I am of purpose, poise, and conviction. Although I lost my marriage, some friends, and my home, had my money stolen from my bank account, and several other things, I feel like I have gained the world. Never underestimate the alchemizing resiliency of a heart that chooses love.

I have allowed my heart to open again to receive love and blessings, and as a result I have soul-nourishing connections in my life which mirror back my core truths and values. When I realized the resilient power of my heart and chose to hone into that power, incredible opportunities came flooding into my life, including soulmate connections with incredible people, amazing clients, opportunities to be featured in places to share my heart with the world, two book deals and counting, the ability to make choices that honor my soul, and an endless supply of laughter, joy, and lightheartedness.

Living with the belief that everything is happening *for* me instead of *to* me has changed my worldview. Wherever you may be today on your journey, remember these truths: you are beautiful beyond measure and you are more than enough. God's plan for your life is greater than anything you could have fathomed for yourself. Love always wins. The spiritual journey is the relinquishment or unlearning of fear and the acceptance of love back into our hearts. You have the power to turn your greatest weakness into your favorite superpower, and empower others to do the same. Fear controls; love surrenders. If you don't know which way to go, I can assure you that when you lead with love, you can't go wrong.

I AM OPEN TO LOVE
IN ALL ITS FORMS.

CHAPTER 13

Standing Strong

*"The one thing you can control is yourself.
You have to love yourself first before you
let another person in."*

BY: CORINNE WALSH STRATTON

Corinne Walsh Stratton

ig: @Corinne_thebean

CORINNE WALSH STRATTON IS incredibly excited to make her publishing debut with such a phenomenal group of women.

She is a wife, mother, blogger, artist, quilter, and the world's most average runner.

She is incredibly proud of her career path, starting out studying theater and costume design and winding up as a physician assistant in orthopedic surgery. She holds bachelor's degrees in both theater arts and health science and a master's of physician assistant studies.

Corinne resides in Central Massachusetts with her wonderful husband, fiery daughter, and tiny dog.

ON THE DAY SHE WAS BORN, the medical staff warned me not to expect her to cry. She was too small, and it was too early. It was not her time yet. They rushed me into the cold, sterile operating room, and the world around me became eerily quiet as the doctor worked quickly to bring her safely into this world. The minutes stretched into eternity as I fought to keep consciousness. Then suddenly, a shriek rang out in the room. She took her first breath and let out a piercing scream. In that moment, she made me a mother. I turned my head to her father and told him to listen to that scream — from that moment on, I knew she would be a force to be reckoned with.

I want to tell my daughter a story about learning to be strong. I want to tell her about all that transpired to bring her into being. Because someday she might have to be stronger than she thinks she could ever be, and I hope she knows that she already has that strength in her.

I had my heart broken for the first time when I was nineteen. We were high school sweethearts and far too young to understand just how much we were supposed to grow and change on our way to adulthood. Promises were made to each other we simply could not keep. We swore to each other we would be together forever and we made that promise work for three years, through the major change that is starting college. It almost destroyed me when he broke that promise, tossing me aside the first time another girl showed him any attention. It took years for me to recover from that betrayal.

After college, I set out on my own for once and moved back to my home city. I made friends, I worked on transitioning my career, and I generally enjoyed being young and single. Then one day, a man came crashing into my life. He was tall, well-educated, and held an impressive job in his career field. He was so far removed from the college guys of my past that he swept me off my feet. I felt like I was in a true adult relationship. We could talk for hours about just about anything. We were in constant communication and spent every available moment together.

The two of us bonded over mutual interests. It was everything I had been waiting for my whole life. The best part was how encouraging he was of my journey to transition career fields and get into my dream graduate degree program.

For three years, he was the most important player in my life. We talked about our future, where we would live, when we would have kids, what we wanted to do with our lives. It seemed like everything was perfect. Being in love clouded my judgement about what was going on. I wanted us to settle down, build a home together, and get married. Despite the fact that he was older, he seemed less in a rush to make these things happen. What had started out as support for my future slowly morphed into putting me down for not having a master's degree or an established career to brag about. Over time, his comments became more derogatory and consistent about how I dressed and the friends I had. There was nothing wrong per se, but I was led to believe that I was young and immature and that I was not someone to show off to his work colleagues and other friends. I was blinded by my love and I thought I had to change to make myself into the person he would want to marry.

One crisp autumn day, I came back to my apartment for a rare night off. I had grabbed take-out and planned a relaxing night of watching movies and probably a bit of studying. When I signed on to my computer, I noticed the red notification icon on my Facebook messenger.

"I don't know the exact nature of your relationship, but I felt strongly that if you are dating him and have been under the impression that you two have been in an exclusive relationship, then you needed to know what was actually going on behind your back . . ."

I think I can recall hearing my heart break as I read those words. The moment is frozen in time: I remember where I was sitting the exact second that my world shattered; the second I realized that the life I had planned out was a complete illusion; the second I realized that the one person I loved more than anything had not only just betrayed me but had also been lying to me for every second of our relationship. The woman from Facebook was not alone. It turned out there were multiple other women, other relationships going on behind my back. I was twenty-six years old when I found myself completely and utterly alone.

After three years, countless *I-love-yous*, and everything I had done to change myself for him, I found myself on my couch with tears streaming down my face. *How could this be happening? How could he have done this to me? How could I have missed that this was going on behind my back?* I was heartbroken and humiliated at the same time.

I thought I had already lived through the great heartbreak of my life when I lost my high school sweetheart. I could not believe I was reliving the experience. This time was different. I had not just been cheated on, but I had also been manip-ulated into a relationship that never really existed. Was I the girlfriend who got cheated on, or was I the other woman?

Growing up, I never would have thought that I would be a woman to end up in an abusive relationship. I could not imagine a situation in which I would let a man call me a terrible name, throw me against a wall, or slap me across the face. Now I know that abuse can take on a much more insidious shape. Abuse can set in so subtly that you do not even recognize it until it has taken root in your relationship and poisoned everything it has touched. I found myself in love with a man who had destroyed my heart and my confidence. When I approached him, he claimed that he *did* love me and would do whatever it took to make our relationship work. I wanted so desperately to be married. To me, marriage meant love and security. I was tired of living with roommates, working for minimal pay, and generally waiting for my life to begin. The thought of having to go back out alone and single was worse than anything else. Who would even want me?

For the briefest of moments, it seemed easier to just stay with him and try to build the trust back, but in my heart I truly could not forgive him for what he had done, and I certainly could not forget it. A few weeks after the explosive revelation, I left the city for a pre-planned trip with a friend. We were headed to the West Coast to see the sights and visit her family. I had never been to the Northwest, and she had been kind enough to invite me along. During the trip, I decided that I wanted to explore Seattle, so I rented myself a room for two days while she spent time with her family. I visited the Space Needle and the museums and walked all over the city, all on my own. I ordered take-out and ate in my room, all on my own. I took photos and ordered a coffee from the original Starbucks. In going through these motions, I began to realize that I *could* do this on my own. I could live my life without him, without the pain he had caused, and without wor-rying whether it would happen again.

As I spent this time alone, I had an enormous revelation about myself. I thought about the nineteen-year-old girl I had been the first time my heart was broken and the sixteen-year-old girl I had been who just wanted to find someone to love her. Somehow, I knew I would have a daughter someday. And I thought about telling her how her father and I met and about how we fell in love. I thought about how I would counsel her through her first heartbreak and what I would tell her from my life experiences. In that moment, I could not imagine looking her in the face and telling her that the best thing she deserved was a man who lied to and cheated on her. I could not tell her she should wipe away her tears, forgive him, and try to move past whatever he had done. Rather, I imagined just stroking her hair and telling her the story of how I brushed myself off and stood strong in my belief in myself. I imagined telling her that she would be able to move on and love herself and that in doing so, she would bring true love into her own life. But first I had to believe that of myself. I had to start believing all those things my mother had been saying since I was young.

I came home from this trip a changed woman. My first step was to extract the toxic person from my life. The only way to do this was to make a clean break, and part of that break meant that I would never have a final conversation with him about removing him from my life. There would never be the apology I deserved or a solid explanation from him as to why this all happened and how he could justify treating me like this. One day I simply chose to stop communicating with him. I could never change him, and so I had to change myself.

I met her father in the most unlikely of ways. Dipping my toes back into a social life at the insistence of my amazing sister, I anticipated having to kiss a lot more frogs. Instead, my sister and brother dragged me out of the house one night, and I ended up talking long into the night with the first guy who walked through the door. We had both experienced bad breakups in the previous year and I thought he would be a nice guy to go out with, temporarily. This time, things unfolded differently. We took a long time to get to know each other. We were friends first without promises to one another. I got to know his friends and got to learn about his true character. He did not hide me away or try to change me.

For the first time in my life, I found myself in love with a man who was not only kind and good, but who also was not serving as an external source of my self-worth. I was loving myself organically, and not using my relationship to fill a void inside. When we stood under the *chuppah* to make our marriage vows a few years later, I knew I had made the right decision to hold out for someone I could not only love but also trust explicitly.

My pregnancy was just about as easy as I could ever imagine. I had no morning sickness, no back pain, and never missed a day of work until my routine thirty-two-week appointment. My feet had swelled over the last week, but I thought that was normal for the third trimester. Then the medical assistant took my blood pressure, and I knew something was wrong. Years of working in medicine had trained me to know even without using a stethoscope that my blood pressure was far too high. And I knew it was a bad sign when my doctor came in to recheck the number two more times. I was heading straight to the hospital. My blood pressure was climbing dangerously high, and there were early signs that the baby was in distress. I was admitted directly to the hospital, and before long teams of medical professionals were streaming into the room. When I was hooked up to an IV to prevent me from having seizures, it felt like fire was dripping into my veins. The neonatal team came in and asked if we had a name for our baby. They were preparing me for her arrival into the world in the next few hours. My blood pressure continued to rise. Knowing my medical background, the nurses turned all the monitors away from me to keep me from panicking over the steadily rising number. My kidneys began to fail, fluid backed up into my lungs, and I was swollen all over.

In a quiet moment in between the tests and exams by various specialists, my mom sat at my bedside. I was trying to be stoic, but she told me it was okay to cry, and for the first time I broke down. I felt like I had failed my baby. My first responsibility as a mother was to bring her safely into this world, and I was failing her. I had done everything to give her the best start in life. I had waited to find the best husband for me and daddy for her. I had been healthy right up until the moment I was not. None of that seemed to matter as I lay in a hospital bed trying to keep her safe inside me a bit longer.

The medical team prepared us for the worst as I got sicker and sicker. Before long, I was rushed to the operating room, the sickest I have ever been. I could not even hold my head up to get an epidural and I clung to the nurse as she held me up. I felt myself fighting for every breath, fighting to stay conscious. And then I heard the most glorious sound in the world as my baby girl took her first breath and let out a strong cry.

From that moment on, I knew we would be okay. From the moment I held her, my heart filled with an incredible new kind of love, and I knew that everything I had fought through was worth it. There are things that happen in life that are out of your control. There are events in life that break your heart. But the one thing you can control is yourself. You have to love yourself first before you let another person in. And when you do let someone in, you still have to command respect for yourself. No one can or should make you feel less than. No one should tell you to settle for "just okay." You can be stronger than you ever realized, no matter what life throws at you. You need to stand strong.

I ALLOW CHANGE
TO IMPROVE ME
EFFORTLESSLY.

CHAPTER 14

My Boyfriend Is Having a Baby

"The universe always had a plan to make me a mother."

By: Jess Reidell

Jess Reidell

http://bit.ly/Mystic_Lemonade (Private Facebook Group)

ig: @agelessjess | fb: @jess.reidell | li: @jessreidell

. . . .

JESS REIDELL IS an Intuitive Life Coach, passionate stage actress, Oracle Card aficionado, and lover of all things mystical and magical. She loves humor, dogs, comedy improvisation, and big glasses of bold red wine. Since 1992, her wish whenever she throws a coin into a fountain or blows out her birthday candles has been "To always have a great time, no matter what."

Jess left corporate America in 2016 to become a Coach after she had an epiphany when her husband asked her on her forty-fifth birthday how it felt to be "halfway to ninety." She now helps her clients break free of the corporate "golden handcuffs" in order to become entrepreneurs or design their own soul-aligned careers. She loves helping others tap into their own intuition, genius, and magic, and she believes the world is a better place when women stop competing with one another and instead cheer each other on and lift each other up.

Jess grew up in the Caribbean on the island of Jamaica. She received her bachelor's degree from Roanoke College in Salem, Virginia and her master's degree in theater performance from Louisiana State University. She currently lives in Atlanta, Georgia with her husband Dave, teenage son Max, and mischievous American Eskimo rescue dog, Cinco.

"I'M EXPECTING A CHILD," HE SAID. "With my ex-girlfriend. That's why I can't take this trip with you. The baby's due in six weeks. I need to be here. I can't leave town."

I sat in stunned silence at the dinner table across from my new boyfriend. The man I had been dating for a little over two months. The one in whose bed I had been waking up four or five days a week. The man who invited me to bring my dog with me when I came to sleep over and who woke up to take her out and let me sleep in.

The man I knew I was falling in love with.

I had not yet said it out loud. I was too guarded and scared to utter the words, "I love you" to his face. That's why I had invited him to take a weekend away in Biloxi, one of my favorite vacation spots. I envisioned a romantic weekend when I could finally speak my truth about my feelings.

I stared down at the meal he had prepared for me. Some fancy recipe from an old *Bon Appetit* magazine. Scallops with tomato avocado coulis and whipped potatoes. It was delicious, but I was confused by the whole scene.

Two nights prior, we had had the strangest date ever. I had told Dave about a restaurant I wanted to try, and I noticed his energy and demeanor changed. He mumbled something in an angry tone about not being able to afford my "expensive tastes." He continued to be distant at dinner, acting like an asshole in fact, and I wondered where the sweet man who had been cracking jokes, courting me, and treating me like a princess had gone.

I paid for dinner that night to make some sort of a point, even though I am still not sure what I was trying to articulate. When we got back to his place he invited me to stay, but for the first time since we began seeing each other, I said no and went home.

The next day I woke up puzzled. *What in the actual hell?* I was thirty-two years old. I had been single for four years since my heartbreaking divorce at twenty-eight. In my two years of going rogue on my dating life, including internet dating back in 2003, long before it was remotely close to being fashionable, I had been on countless first dates and a handful of second dates. There were two re-lationships that had lasted three months or less and one that lasted a few months more, which resulted in an engagement before I gave the ring back because every cell in my body knew that it wasn't the right thing. This was the *first man* I had actually *fallen for* in *four fucking years*. I had never intended to fall at all. When we met, I had been so jaded from all the goal-directed and outcome-oriented dating and failed relationships that I said to myself, "He's totally cute. I can't wait to sleep with him. This will probably last about a month."

I needed answers. I picked up the phone and called him.

"Is everything okay?" I asked. "You weren't yourself last night. What's going on with you?"

All he said was, "Come over tonight. I'll make you dinner." Then he hung up.

Dinner? What in the actual fuck? Is he cooking me dinner so he can break up with me? What do you wear to a "break-up" dinner? Should I bring the dog?

I pondered these things.

Flash forward again to the scallops-with-some-fancy-kinda-coulis-I'm-having-a-baby-with-another-woman-so-I-can't-go-to-Biloxi-with-you dinner. I grabbed my wine glass and took a big gulp of chardonnay. We sat for a few minutes in stony silence. Finally, I spoke.

"Why didn't you tell me about this sooner?" I asked.

"It's not the kind of thing you bring up on a first date," he said.

"You're right," I said. "If you had shared this on our first date, it would have been our last. I might have just escaped through the bathroom window."

He ignored my comment. "I am crazy about you," he said. "I would love to be in a relationship with you. I *want* to go to Biloxi with you. I want to take you to Italy . . ."

"But I know how this must feel," he continued. "If my sister came to me in this situation, I would throw her some running shoes and tell her to run, so I under-stand if you need to go."

I didn't leave his house that night. I stayed. It was very uncharacteristic of the self I knew. It was surreal, like being in a romantic comedy after there's been a major plot twist. We talked more, and he filled in some of the blanks. They were already broken up when they had the indiscretion. He thought she was still on the pill. After he found out, he made it very clear that they broke up for a reason and that he did not think they should be together, but he told her that he would support her in whatever decision she made. I remember lying with my head in his lap as he stroked my hair. I remember the heavy spaces of silence in our strained conversation.

"Is it a boy or a girl?" I finally asked, numbly.

"It's a boy," he said. "We're going to name him Max."

The next morning, I woke up with a sense of clarity. I wanted space. I needed it in order to regain some perspective.

Over coffee, I looked at Dave and said, "I need to process this some more. And I'm going to date other people. Before this came up, I never would have dreamed of doing that, but there are some other people interested in me and I think I owe it to myself to give them a chance."

He nodded. A few nights later, I went on a date with another man I had met on the dating website. His screen name was "Disco Hoss." I had found it amusing.

The day after the date with "Disco Hoss," Dave surprised me at work. He brought a bouquet of flowers and asked to take me to lunch. He was staring at me as though I were the most beautiful woman he had ever laid eyes on. Essentially, he was staking his claim. I'll admit it was all quite charming.

Can I do this? I asked myself. *When there's about to be a child in the picture changing up the whole idyllic vision of my relationship that had been forming in my enchanted imagination?*

Yes, came the whisper from my intuition. *Give it three months, then ask again.*

I took the trip to Biloxi by myself. It was bittersweet. I ruminated on my current reality and gambled and drank way too many cosmopolitans. I imagined how things might have been different if we had met prior to this coming to pass.

One night after I was back, a call came in on Dave's phone. It was time to take a midnight trip to the hospital. Nothing quite like lying next to your boyfriend in bed when he gets *that* phone call and leaves to take his expectant ex to labor and delivery. I remember the energy of his voice, nervous excitement with a touch of fear, and thinking about how marvelously he was handling himself and how nothing about this situation could be easy for him either.

Before daylight, he crawled back into bed next to me. "False alarm," he said, kissing my forehead.

"Any day now," I mumbled and drifted back to sleep, thinking of how surreal it all was.

Max made his debut about two weeks later, on June 16, 2003. After his first six weeks on the planet, he would spend every other weekend with us at Dave's. While still a screaming infant, Max fascinated my dog Sugar, who was fiercely protective of this new little creature. That was sweet to watch. It was also sweet to watch what a "hands on" dad Dave was. As Max squealed angrily during his diaper change, I would overhear Dave talking to him, acting as though it were a conversation:

"Wow! And then what happened?"

More loud squeals.

"And what happened after that?"

It was too cute.

Cute as it all was, though, the future loomed ahead. I found myself in a new year with both a man and a child in my life, and with another woman, the child's mother, still wanting my boyfriend to be with her. That was an uncomfortable space. I resisted getting more attached to the child. As for the man, I was head over heels in love.

Every three months, I would ask myself the question, "Given these circumstances, can I *really* do this?" I listened to my intuition for the answer. And the answer that whispered back was always *yes*.

Before learning of Max's impending arrival, I told Dave that I would not be likely to date someone beyond a year's time if marriage wasn't in the cards. If someone didn't know if I was "the one" within a year, I was fairly confident I wasn't. I reminded him of this and shared my concerns about getting more attached to Max.

"Is this an ultimatum?" Dave asked.

"Not exactly," I said. "It's what I want. If it's not what you want, I'll be *hurt*, I'll be *sad*, but I will move on to find what *I* want. I'd rather know now, before too much time passes."

And in a moment of complete clarity, standing in my truth, I looked my love in the eye and said: "Consider your life with me, and consider it without me, and decide what you would prefer."

He proposed one month later.

Onward into parenthood we went, not knowing exactly how to proceed, seeing as it was uncharted territory for both of us. We were weekend warrior parents. There were bottles, bath time and bedtime rituals, and a big book about babies that we would consult periodically. I'll never forget one weekend when Max was around seven months old and just wouldn't stop screaming. *What? Why?* I asked myself. He was changed and dry, he had taken his bottles. I consulted the book.

"Your baby should have a mixture of formula and/or breast milk and solid foods at this stage," I read aloud to Dave.

Solid foods? Fucking solid foods? Holy God, how had we missed this?

We freaked out and started feeding him everything in the house: yogurt, cheese, sliced strawberries and plums. He made it very clear what he liked and disliked with super-dramatic facial expressions that cracked us both up. To this day, I think he picked up his flair for the dramatic from me, the actress.

The pleasure of preparing and eating food became a big theme in our family. After Dave and I married, when Max was around three, we received a full miniature child's kitchen so he could bang around in it while were cooking dinner. Once he was a little older, we had him helping with food prep and taught him to chop vegetables (with strict supervision, of course). On the weekends he was with us, I would carefully plan fun meals to cook together. I loved creating excitement around food. "Guess what we're having for dinner?" was my favorite question.

When Max was around five and a half, he suddenly looked at me and Dave and announced, "We need to have a little *girl!*" Dave and I glanced at each other. It was serendipitous timing because I had recently gone off the pill and we were trying to make a baby. But I was thirty-eight. Time was not on our side.

"We would like that, too," Dave said, awkwardly. "And we are making some efforts to make that happen, okay? But it isn't for sure. Do you understand?"

It wasn't for sure. We had declared that there would be no heroic efforts on our part to get pregnant, no in vitro or fancy fertility treatments. After five years of trying, Dave and I had a heart-to-heart talk and we both agreed it was time to let it be. At the age of forty-three, the idea of pregnancy and a newborn baby now felt scarier than it was exciting.

The universe had always had a plan to make me a mother. It gave me the ultimate privilege of being a second mom to this beautiful boy. I got the chance to read him bedtime stories and take him shopping. We went to the movies, museums, and on family vacations. We tricked him into liking broccoli by ordering it with butter at a restaurant before our main meal and making a big show of how yummy it was — that trick worked so well that broccoli is still his favorite vegetable to this day.

I got to teach him the little life lessons that helped me as a kid, like how important it was to try foods you were not sure if you would like and how even if you tasted it and decided you really didn't like it you could put it on the fork with something you liked better to make it more palatable.

I taught him how important it is to always look people in the eye, to be a good sport even when you lose at a game, to always tell the truth, and to never cry wolf so you would be considered trustworthy. This particular lesson happened to be extra difficult for me and involved one of those toy alligators that grows to several times its size when you soak it in water. Over a Christmas holiday when Max was five years old, I was surprised to find such an alligator in one of our toilets. When I confronted him, he denied it.

"Come on now," I said. "Tell the truth." More vigorous head shaking, denying, and looking down at his feet.

I got down on his level and looked him straight in the eye. Here came the hard part.

"I'm going to ask you *one more time*. And this is your opportunity to tell me the truth. Look me in the eye. *Did you put the alligator in the toilet*?" The words sounded ridiculous, and it was a struggle not to laugh; however, I remained reverent and poker-faced, knowing how important this moment was as a disciplinarian.

"Yes. I put the alligator in the toilet," he said, breaking my gaze and looking down in shame.

I softened a bit but remained serious.

"Thank you for telling the truth. The truth is the most important thing. Even if you think you are in trouble, you always make things ten times worse by lying."

This was one of my tougher solo disciplinarian moments. Thankfully, Dave and I agreed on most our parenting strategies, and we always showed a united front in Max's presence. It made disciplining him so much easier because we always had each other's backs.

In time, things got much better with Max's mother. We would all show up for parent-teacher conferences, we collaborated on Halloween costumes, and we spent Easters together as a joint holiday. We celebrated his confirmation together, and his eighth-grade graduation. It takes a village, and we had one.

Over time, Max has become a great little chef. I always joke that his dad taught him the art of timing and I taught him the art of infusing food with love. It came as no surprise when at age eleven, he got excited to audition for *MasterChef Junior*. Apprehensive at first, he ultimately decided to take a year to perfect his craft and get better at cooking. He auditioned the following year and was a great sport when he wasn't chosen as a finalist. I would proudly display the meals he prepared on Facebook, and when people asked how he could create those fancy meals, his proud response was always "I learned from the best."

We raised Max to be a little gentleman. I always get my car door opened and my grocery bags carried for me. As I type this, he is fifteen and is making broiled salmon for us while Dave is away traveling. We have dinner together as a family every Tuesday, even if it's just the two of us because Dave is out of town. After dinner, he will drive us back to his other house, and we always make a point to say, "I love you."

I know stepmothers sometimes get a bad rap or don't enjoy their role, but I couldn't be more thrilled with the life I chose. I have been in Max's life from the very beginning, and I've grown to love him more with each year that passes. It doesn't matter to me what anyone says; even though I did not give birth to him — he will always be my son.

LOVE IS A CHOICE.

CHAPTER 15

No Words Needed

"I believe when people say love heals all wounds, because I've seen miraculous signs of proof."

BY: MARYANN PERRI

Maryann Perri

ig: @maryannperri l fb: @maryannperri

MARYANN PERRI IS A self-proclaimed "super-mom" with a big heart and an empathetic approach toward people. She is an overachiever with an abundance of energy and an overzealous love for life and adventure. A graduate of York University with a post-graduate diploma from Seneca College, she majored in corporate communications, landing several exciting jobs along the way. She married her high school sweetheart in 2002 and soon after moved to Mexico, where she dedicated herself to teaching English. Fourteen years, three kids, two dogs, and an entire new circle of friends later, Maryann mastered speaking Spanish and developed a love for the Mexican culture, food, people, and country.

Maryann's husband and her children, Cristian, Mia, and Alexia, are her pride and joy. Full of spunk, laughter, and passion, Maryann deems life to be an adventure that one must continuously challenge. She always fills the room with her big personality and believes we are not meant to live in a "square box"; rather, we must take chances to add zest and variety to our journey. She feels change is necessary for our development as human beings. Her goal is to drive people to find their happiness. "Everything happens for a reason" is her mantra, and she has found that tragedy has allowed her to see the good in every situation. In her free time, Maryann loves to cook, travel, exercise, read, and spend quality time with her friends, family, husband, and children.

I REMEMBER LIKE IT WAS YESTERDAY, embedded in my mind forever — that feeling you get in the pit of your stomach when you're watching a suspense movie. Your breathing gets faster and you're petrified, sitting at the edge of your seat, as you cover your eyes waiting anxiously for what's about to happen next. This one day was just like that: traumatic, reflective, life-altering. Only it wasn't a horrific scene from a movie, it was my life as I had known it for thirty-seven years that was changing.

On November 4, 2014, my dad had a stroke.

I remember our last phone call, our last conversation. I was waiting for my kids to get home from school, cooking and chatting on the phone with my dad, as I regularly did.

"Dad, are you sure you don't want to meet us in Mexico for Cristian's annual soccer tournament?" We lived abroad at the time, but he never missed a tournament. He loved watching his first-born grandson play soccer, but this time he told me he couldn't.

"I have a lot of work to do, maybe next year!" he said.

I thought it was strange — he clearly had a premonition, perhaps a feeling that something bad was about to happen. His intuition was right: next year would not be possible. This would be our last father-daughter conversation.

Sometimes I think morbid thoughts, questioning my life span and wondering if I'll be around long enough to see my kids get married, or hold my grandchildren, or grow old with my husband by my side. Life can change in a nanosecond. Our world as we know it can change *drastically* from one moment to the next, in a blink of an eye. That's why it is so important to love passionately while we can and to genuinely appreciate the value of love reciprocated back to us.

An hour after we got off the phone, I got that dreadful call. The call that changed my family's life forever. My dad had suffered an ischemic stroke. Thankfully he survived, but everything changed from that point forward. Not only were his motor skills affected, but he also lost his ability to speak.

What would you do if you saw one of your parents in the most vulnerable and helpless state? What would you do if you had to help your parents in a way they did for you when you were young, knowing their pride is at stake but you have no other choice? I've had to. And as I willingly try and help my dad out of certain situations due to his current disability, I often look deep into his eyes and feel a dreadful pang of pain in the pit of my stomach. I feel his sadness and know he's so desperately trying to tell me something — but he can't.

I'm angry. I'm broken. I'm devastated. I miss my dad, as he was.

I miss our chats, his annoying jokes to which my response would be, more often than not, "Dad, stop! Be quiet!"

Why? Why did I tell him to be quiet? I so desperately wish I could take those words back! I so desperately wish I could have a conversation with my father like we used to.

We all have memories of our childhood. Some are fond memories; others are not so happy. My memories are of playing in the yard or smelling fresh cut grass — always a reminder that Daddy was home. We were happy. He would chase us around with the sprinkler or kick the soccer ball for us to catch. He loved soccer, he always loved to kick the ball around with us. Only now, he can't.

I remember lying next to my dad on a beach chair in our yard when I was around five or six years old, pretending he was my prince. I loved my dad to pieces and I always looked up to him — he was my knight in shining armor and was always there to protect me, to take care of me.

Those are my memories.

He was funny. Sarcastic. Stubborn. Kind-hearted. Hard-working.

Life hasn't been all that easy for my family. Like most, we've had many challenges thrown our way. We've had to climb steep mountains and overcome some very difficult moments. Sometimes I wonder if all the stress contributed to my father's present state, many years later.

Back in 1991, my family lost everything to a shameless group of thieves who stole my father's business and robbed me and my sister of a happy and carefree childhood. We struggled financially and emotionally, starting when I was only sixteen years old, as we watched our parents battle the hardships couples face when they have no air to breathe and can't seem to escape the waves crashing over them. "What doesn't kill you makes you stronger," I would repeat to myself.

It's the worst thing to see your loved ones — your parents — go from happy to devastated within seconds. Life changed. We changed. I changed who I was, but I became who I am today because of it. It's funny how one incident in your life can modify its direction indefinitely, defining who you will be for the rest of your life and what will become of your destiny. We were young when my family lost everything, but old enough to know things would never be the same. I remember vividly my father crying as I hugged him and tried to comfort him. He was inconsolable. I had never seen my father so weak and helpless until history repeated itself again years later, in a different way. I had never known what it was like to be the daughter taking the role of the caregiver. Hugging him tightly, my goal was to make him feel everything would be okay. Whether I believed it or not has always remained a mystery, and in a strange twist of fate, just over twenty years later I have again become the caregiver.

When my dad suffered his stroke, I was living abroad, so I quickly made my way to Toronto to be by his side. Walking into the hospital room and seeing him helpless on a gurney, staring at the ceiling as if thinking, "What just happened to me?" — that was a sight I will never forget. I tried so hard to hold back my tears and to be the pillar of strength my family needed. I held his hand gently and once again told him everything would be okay, but I really wasn't sure. He cried when he saw me, and I was overcome with so much grief, so much emotion. This was my dad laying there: my knight in shining armor had been defeated. I was devastated.

The prognosis was grim. They told us the first seventy-two hours would be critical, and the doctors didn't know if he would pull through. By the third day, we could somewhat help him sit up, but not without watching him impotently topple over again. It mortified me to see my father, who was always so strong, look powerless. As the days passed, we were given a despairing outlook of what life would be like from that moment forward. Praying for a miracle was our only hope.

They told us he would never walk again. It took a lot of encouragement and love from us to make him believe he could, and ultimately, he would. My dad's lifelong love of soccer and the strength of his once-athletic legs turned out to be blessings that gave him the force and encouragement he needed.

"You got this, Dad, you *will* walk again, just keep trying!"

"Your legs are strong and have always been! You need to kick the soccer ball around with your grandchildren again!"

He took about a month, but he walked, slowly.

They also told us he would never speak again. My dad has conditions called global aphasia and apraxia.

Global aphasia is a severe impairment of both expressive and receptive skills and is usually associated with a large left hemisphere lesion. People with global aphasia are often alert and may be able to express themselves through facial expressions, intonation, and gestures.[6]

Apraxia is a poorly understood neurological condition. People who have it find it difficult or impossible to make certain motor movements, even though their muscles are normal. With apraxia of speech, a person finds it difficult or impossible to move his or her mouth and tongue to speak. This happens even though the person has the desire to speak and the mouth and tongue muscles can physically form words.[7]

Severe global aphasia and apraxia erases a person's communication abilities in their entirety, kind of like when your laptop goes haywire and all of your stored files vanish. Well, that's what happened. My father lost the ability to speak and write. We have tried many different tactics using iPads, images, and special therapies, to no avail. This means there has been significant damage to the left frontal lobe of his brain.

While I was still living in Mexico, I arranged for my dad to stay with us for a few months, trying everything and anything possible to help. From hyperbaric oxygen therapy to physical rehabilitation, I tried hard. I would spend hours playing dominoes with him to help match numbers and colors. I would help him write his name and write numbers consecutively while he tried to fill in the blanks. I know he knew how much we wanted to help, and I know he felt that love was all around him, constantly.

I often try to imagine what it must feel like. To be fully present physically but unable to take part in any conversation. Imagine yourself wanting so badly to say something, but you can't. You're unable to use your words. You can only think of them and no one around you can hear your screams from the inside. People assume you are trying to say one thing when in reality you have something different in mind. You can't express yourself. You are a living, breathing, walking person with no ability to communicate.

I always tell my mom to be grateful for what you have now and to stop dwelling on what you lost. She's suffered the most from all that has happened, and I sometimes catch her in deep sorrow, grieving the loss of the man she married all those years ago and watching the new "him" struggle on a daily basis. I have had to let my faith take over. I've had several conversations with God, pleading for just about anything, any sign of hope. I believe God undeniably answered my prayers and has sent us a significant message through my father.

The day my dad uttered his first meaningful words post-stroke, we were at home playing a game of dominos. By playing, I mean I lay the dominos face up and had my dad try placing the numbers consecutively and by color. At times he gets it, and at times he doesn't. My outlook on his inabilities has been to take a humorous approach and make him laugh as much as possible. I will tell him secrets or things my kids have told me (that no one should know), and I finish with, "But don't *tell* anyone, Daddy!" and we both laugh together. Playing dominos on that very special day, I began with my silly banter while I watched him laugh at my ridiculous jokes. He giggled and I casually told him how much I love him, as I always did and continue to do. That's when he suddenly responded with the words, "I love you!" I was astounded. Overwhelmed. I couldn't believe what I had just heard! *My father who couldn't speak just told me he loves me!* I remember the moment so clearly. I choked up and tried so very hard not to cry — but this time with tears of joy. Normally, with aphasia and apraxia, patients are unable to repeat a word. I said it again.

"I love you, Dad!"

And he repeated again, "I love you!"

The only words my dad is able to repeat on demand and use correctly and at the appropriate times are "I love you." *Remarkable! A miracle? Some kind of divine intervention in which the force of his love for his family granted him the ability to give us this gift? Perhaps.* At that very moment, I felt there was hope. Although some people may think these seem like too few and too small words to rejoice, these small words mean more to me than anyone can ever imagine. I can hear my father tell me he loves me again! Nothing can ever replace that. Though at times I feel I should have done more for him and a sense of failure kicks in, I remind myself that love is all the hope we have left. When all the odds were against us, being mindful of these small miracles has kept me at peace and kept my dad by my side.

We don't know if my father will ever speak again. We do know he still has his pride and that he understands everything that goes on around him. He laughs with us frequently, and he cries on his own often. He cries because he is frustrated at his inability and incompetence. His independence has been taken away from him forever. His hands don't work like they used to — those hands were once his livelihood and they created and designed so many beautiful coats, vests, and pillows over the years. The hands that guided mine when I was a little girl now need mine to help guide them.

I don't cry in front of my dad, nor do I cry in front of my mom. I keep my composure around my sister not because I try to be a martyr but because I try to take a positive approach and hope it becomes contagious. Hope is all we have left, and our love and bond as a family has helped him through some of the most difficult of times. Our union as a family has never been stronger. We have supported each other and helped one another through some tough moments.

I've often heard that love comes in many forms. I *strongly* believe this powerful force of nature is the reason behind all the small miracles we have seen take place since my dad had his stroke. I believe when people say love heals all wounds, because I've seen miraculous signs of proof along the path of my dad's journey.

My heart is full. I realize things will never be the same, but I am grateful we still get to hold his hand. We are blessed to receive his special tight hugs and listen to his laughter at our silly jokes. He smiles at his grandkids and is always prepared to snuggle and give kisses. He listens intently when we speak (just as he always did) about life and about our own personal challenges. We take his advice by assuming what he would say if he had use of his words and by the look in his beautiful green eyes. I am grateful because I strongly believe our devotion strengthened his fight to be here, only slightly modified, with a minor glitch in his abilities and a heart filled with so much love.

"I love you too, Daddy . . ."

EVERYTHING IS ALWAYS WORKING OUT FOR ME.
I AM SAFE AND I AM TAKEN CARE OF.
I GIVE MYSELF PERMISSION TO RELAX
RIGHT HERE AND RIGHT NOW.

CHAPTER 16

Unconventional Love

"Your age does not define or limit your ability to love."

BY: TAMARA SIMPERS

Tamara Simpers

TAMARA IS IN CONSTANT PURSUIT of reinventing herself to achieve her dreams. She is currently pursuing a doctoral degree in clinical psychology from the California School of Professional Psychology. As a graduate student, she has provided psychotherapy to incarcerated women and finds this work immensely rewarding. She has also completed clinical training in community mental health and community college settings. Tamara is interested in growing as a clinician, a professional, and a person. In doing so, she strives to learn more about various areas of mental health and social justice.

Tamara also works hard to maintain a balance between her roles as student, clinician, wife, mother, stepmother, daughter, sister, and friend. She believes in the healing effects of spirituality and connection to community. She takes part in activities that rejuvenate her spirit, such as cycling, swimming, hiking, and spending time with her family. Additionally, she enjoys jury duty, collecting picnic baskets, and meditating with her cat. Her previous career was in mortgage lending, where she learned about work ethic and sharing goals with a team. Tamara believes that we can use all experiences to cultivate growth, maturity, connection with others, and change. Her goals are to continue evolving as a person and to be a tool of healing for others.

I MET HER IN A DREAM. I saw her beautiful, full cheeky face, her cute pink lips, and her big blue eyes. The days leading up to my delivery felt chaotic and stressful. My relationship with her father was unstable. I worried about how I would be a mother to her while I was struggling with him, but the image I saw of her brought excitement and hope during a tumultuous time.

Discovering Motherhood

I had my daughter when I was eighteen years old. The enormous weight of raising a child when I thought I had nothing to offer felt daunting. I did not understand what type of parent I wanted to be and had no philosophy about what type of family I wanted to have. I had no direction and I was scared to mess up another person's life. Part of me was ashamed for contributing to the statistic of teenage motherhood: I was born to a single mother and was now perpetuating the cycle of becoming a single mother, without a stable home or income. I feared raising my daughter in an environment of struggle and heartache, yet those were the consequences of my experience with teenage love.

I remember our first moments alone together, holding her in the middle of the night while she was crying. I just kept thinking, "What do I do now? What does she need? How does this work?" My initial impression of motherhood was that I wasn't doing it right. Somewhere along the way, I had accepted the negative connotations that came with the label of "teen mom." I perceived my uncertainty, inexperience, and mistakes as the shortcomings of a young mother. Little did I know that my experiences as a new mother were natural. Age does not circumvent the feelings of angst that come with having your first child, nor does it create a flawless and intuitive experience of motherhood. Today I understand motherhood to be a process of constant emotional and spiritual change. It is a blend of nurturing new life and new experiences while not losing oneself. The process is experiential, based on trial and error. However, at the time, I felt like I didn't measure up to what a mom should be.

In the beginning, I relied heavily on guidance from her loving, generous grand-parents. They were my teachers, and their enthusiasm for and connection with my daughter gave me a sense of security. I still struggled to develop my voice as a mother, wavering between following others' examples and listening to my own convictions. I continued to doubt myself and I assumed others knew better than me, but this doubt became more and more uncomfortable to sustain. Eventually, I began to take risks and trust my gut.

Discovering Her

Being a single parent was a rocky road. At times, it felt like the blind leading the blind. She was a fiery, funny, creative, and temperamental little girl — the complete opposite of me as a child. I grew up as the youngest of four children and was mostly dominated by my older siblings. I was passive and always looking for the path of least resistance. My daughter was different: she had a strong spirit about her.

Discovering her was like falling in love — exciting, surprising, and at times con-flicting. I often told her, "The thing that gets you in trouble is also my favorite thing about you." I would describe my role as her parent as if it were a sport; sometimes I played offense, sometimes defense, but I was always in the game even when it was rainy, muddy, and cold and I felt like I was losing. She brought out a passion in me to be the best parent I could be, but that passion often be-came distorted by my desire to be the perfect parent.

My daughter challenged me frequently, not by pushing parent-child boundaries (although she did do that) but by making me learn to parent according to our dif-ferences. I had to parent her based on who she was at the time, not who I thought she should be. That difference was hard to discern and I didn't always get it right.

I wanted her to get straight As when she was in elementary school, and I over-simplified this idea by telling her she was capable and just needed to apply her-self. I thought if I continued to encourage her, she would meet my expectations, but that was not the case. The pressure I put on her created stress, anxiety, and tension for us both. She began to struggle academically, in a constant state of putting out fires regarding her slipping grades. After trying different avenues to support her, I finally took her to a child psychologist. We discovered that she had ADHD, which was affecting her ability to focus and stay attentive to her school work. I felt guilty. Here I was, setting unrealistic expectations for her and giving her consequences when she did not meet them. I had stubbornly dug my heals in and demanded that she tried harder; little did I know she was trying her hardest.

I called my best friend and unloaded all my guilt and shame. I was once again convinced that if I had been a better mom I would have been able to prevent this from happening or recognized it sooner. My best friend, to whom I ran and cried often, was in many ways an unofficial co-parent. I would call her regarding various parenting situations and reason out strategies with her. I would often call her just to say my deepest secret out loud: "I'm doing it wrong." In a way, I wanted her to agree that I was a bad parent, but thankfully she didn't partake in my shaming ritual. Instead, she would remind me of all that I was doing right, I would listen and wipe my tears, and we would make a new plan about how to approach the situation differently.

Somewhere along the way, I subscribed to the idea that my daughter would become the person I sculpted her to be. I thought I had the power and responsibility to set a standard for her that I couldn't even reach myself. Without being aware of it, I was parenting her with the goal of righting my own wrongs. All my mistakes or bad choices would be experiences that she would never have because I would teach her differently. The only problem was that life was not containable, and neither was her spirit. I was trying to spoon-feed her my idea of what life should be instead of allowing her to discover it for herself, even in the smallest of ways. Thankfully, my daughter was not buying into any of my romantic notions, and she expressed herself in her own way, unique to her and different from me.

One morning when I was getting ready to take her to school, she walked out with a typical outfit on of shorts and a shirt. But this time, she added a colorful scarf around her neck. It was beautiful, it was different, and it was something I'd never seen before. This was her version of experiencing life. In turn, my spiritual practice was to let go of my idealistic view of motherhood and instead discover how life would unfold for her in a beautiful, different, never-before-seen kind of way.

Rediscovering Me

Being my daughter's mother was a part of me, but not all of me. Whenever I lost sight of that fact, I unconsciously looked to my daughter to fill the voids. The result was suffocation and rigidity in our relationship, which kept us both from growing. I had dreams before becoming a mother, but I believed they had expired because I now fell outside the traditional timelines. I made rules for myself such as not dating until my daughter was eighteen years old, because I thought that was what would be best for her. I wanted to go back to school to pursue a higher education, but I thought it would be unfair for her to have a mother working and going to school. Inadvertently, I was putting my life on hold and becoming a martyr in the process.

As I grew unhappy with my day job and apologetic for wanting to be in a relationship, I started to poke holes in these ideas by asking questions. *Why wait?*

When I explained to a friend why it would be absurd to go back to school at my age, she simply asked, "What else are you going to do?" This statement made me laugh, but it also scared me to death. It was true — what else *was* I going to do? I was growing bitter and stagnant, trying and perpetually failing to live by the rules I made up for myself.

I enrolled in an undergraduate program and started going to school two nights a week while working. Life seemed messy and hard to juggle at times. I fought feelings of guilt when I was at school instead of at home with my daughter, but I started to reconnect with myself and discover who I was outside of motherhood. I became better equipped to help my daughter with school assignments, and we did homework together many nights.

In taking the terrifying risk to go back to school, I discovered more of myself and allowed myself the opportunity to develop as a person outside of my role as a mother. This process happened outside of the standard societal milestones, as I became a mother before I completely became myself. Simultaneously, as I was developing who I was, my daughter was developing and discovering who she was. My role as her mother changed. I had to become fluid and flexible in order to support her growth.

After a few years, my daughter watched me graduate from college with my bachelor's degree. A couple years later, I watched her graduate from high school and move across country to attend a four-year university. Then I graduated with my master's degree, and she followed with her bachelor's degree. We changed together. We connected around the pursuit of our dreams. We shared this season of hard work, perseverance, faith, accomplishment, and celebration.

I'll never forget saying goodbye when we went to my daughter's freshman orientation at her college campus thousands of miles away. I was proud and excited for her to have an opportunity to attend college out of state. But that first year I suffered, struggling to develop who I was outside of her. My mantra at the time was, "I'm in transition." My friends would ask, "How are you doing? How is she doing?" My response always began with, "I'm in transition." I felt like a cat with its claws anchored into the carpet, looking around to make sure everything is safe before reluctantly letting go. Her freshman year was like an identity crisis for me. I craved our old life together, just the two of us. I had to learn that sometimes the things that are comfortable to us are not always better for us; they are just familiar.

Rediscovering Romance

I received a lot of judgment for being single well into my thirties. My relationship status felt like a raw nerve reminding me that I'd once again fallen behind in attaining the social norms. I craved a loving relationship, but I was cutting my teeth on a lot of superficial relationships that could not understand my unconventional life of being in school and having a teenage daughter. It wasn't until I began to hit my stride being single — not feeling like I needed to answer invasive questions or think that something was wrong with me — that I met my future husband.

He seemed like a breath of fresh air. We met for a business meeting and connected right away over the topic of single parenthood. He was still early in his journey, as his son was a toddler. Our stories aligned in so many ways that it almost felt miraculous. Our common foundation was parenting, and although we decided not to have any children together, we support, advise, and rally around each other as parents. Like many blended families, the transition from a single parent home to a blended home is not always easy and takes nurturing. I get to apply the same spiritual practice with my husband and stepson as I did with my daughter and myself — to allow them the space to discover who they are in their relationship with each other and individually without interfering in the process. It has been challenging at times to know where I fit in, but that usually happens when I am tempted to change the process. I see my role as a wife and stepmother to be a cheerleader, advocate, companion, role model, and ultimately mirror of who they are and who they want to be. They are the same for me.

How She Healed Me

One Mother's Day, I received a card from my daughter. She had just graduated from college and was bursting with excitement and pride about the new opportunities ahead of her. The letter was filled with reflective statements of gratitude for the support she had on her journey and the relationship we have today. She told me how proud she was of me and of us. My eyes welled up with tears at the loving words poured all over the paper. I reflected on past cards with her handmade messages of love: "You're the best mommy ever" or "Thank you for being my mommy." I realized that she has been affirming me as a mother all along; I just couldn't always receive the message.

At times, the busyness of motherhood blinded me to my daughter's loving words, and the loving moments became overshadowed by seemingly more important duties of the day. Other times, my burden of insecurity and guilt as a mother kept me from believing her words. In this moment, reading that card, I could not look away from them. Her words healed the old ideas I had carried for years — that I wasn't a good enough mother, that I was doing it all wrong, that she deserved better. With her words, she put those old ideas to rest. I felt free to accept that my unconventional journey of motherhood is more than good enough. It is loving, passionate, hard fought, unrelenting, and spiritual. Today, I practice feeling proud of who I am as a mother and a person. I accept that both are always changing.

How We've Changed

Today my daughter is a young adult living in Chicago. She is fiercely pursuing dreams of her own while staying curious about who she is. I am continuously inspired by her wisdom in honoring where she is and what she needs. She takes an intuitive and spiritual approach to life and seems to know that she cannot discover who she is when she is restricted by trying to be who people think she should be. She makes decisions accordingly, and in doing so she has a beautiful and simple life.

I live in California and at times I become nervous about my daughter experiencing real winters in the Midwest. I find myself asking, "What kind of jacket do you have? Are you warm enough? How's your car holding up in the snow?" Her responses are minimal and mostly dismissive: "Yes, yes, fine." I want my worry to be contagious so she can take action (like getting a gigantic winter jacket and snow tires) that makes ME feel better. But instead she shares how she's enjoying the winter and thinks it's fun to dig her car out of the snow. Once again, I get the opportunity to see life through her eyes as carefree and adventurous.

My relationship with my daughter is still one of transitions. Managing a long-distance relationship is not always easy. We play phone tag, and when too much time passes without connecting, there are hurt feelings. But overall, we both feel loved and supported by each other. My role as a mother has evolved from a primary caretaker to a provider of unconditional emotional support, free of judgement. I still practice sharing my experiences with her rather than giving advice. But what has changed, is now she wants to hear them.

I used to think that love needed to follow traditional timelines and age requirements to be secure and meaningful. But the love that I have experienced throughout my life has been unconventional and has rebelled against societal norms. This love has come at unexpected times and when I felt least deserving of it. It has transformed my heart and showed me that age does not define or limit our capacity to love.

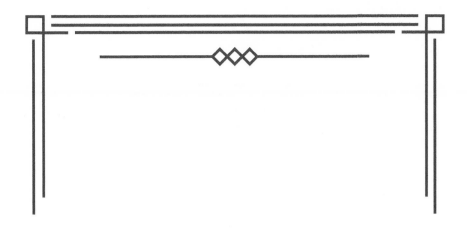

INHALE GRATITUDE.

EXHALE LOVE.

CHAPTER 17

Dearest Captain
of My Heart

---

*"I fell in love with him for all the ways
he made me fall in love with me."*

By: Mandy Valpey

Mandy Valpey

goddessguide1111.com

ig: @goddessguidance1111 | fb: @goddessguide1111

MANDY IS A Goddess Guide Feminine Intuition Expert. She empowers women to reconnect to their feminine core, open their hearts, and trust their innate wisdom so that they may live juicier, more vibrant, and joyful lives. Her clients come from around the world and from all different backgrounds. Together, they address personal and relationship issues, uncover triggers and trauma, and work through self-esteem blocks to discover their deepest desires. Mandy uses the expertise gained from her background in psychology, coupled with her use of empowering language, crystals, chakra balancing techniques, tarot and oracle cards, to help her clients integrate body, mind, and spirit while standing fully rooted in their feminine power. She has studied and practiced yoga and Vipassana meditation in the United States and abroad, has completed certifications in both Tantra and Jñāna yoga, has facilitated *Course in Miracles* groups, and led women's circles in Northern California.

SOUL LOVE — the kind that simultaneously makes your heart skip a beat and feel all fluttery with wonder and excitement, like Bambi taking his first steps. The recognition that even though you may have only just met this beloved creature moments before, you'd know his soul anywhere. That lightning bolt of electric shock recognition you feel with every fiber of your being. I know you. I've played with you lifetimes before. I could never forget your heart, or the deep grooves you've left in the shadows of my soul.

This is the love I know I was born to make. The kind that makes my skin crawl with desire and my toes curl with anticipation, all while my heart aches for the hero's journey — the one that inevitably changes me from the inside out.

Upon seeing his profile picture and swiping right, I knew I had to know this man. We matched on a Saturday afternoon after I had convinced myself I'd never go on another dating app date again, ever. I had even told my roommate so just moments before. Hell, I was not even matching with anyone on any dating apps anymore anyway, so trying seemed a little hopeless. That summer left a labyrinth of discarded flings interspersed with connected moments I hoped would have lasted longer and some less-than-stellar intimate encounters. I thought perhaps it was time to open myself up to the possibilities I know await an open, willing heart.

Only a few weeks from jumping on a plane to Bali, where I was sure I had left my heart in the fall of 2016, I thought, "Why not see what kind of fun or trouble I can get myself into?" I have loved and grown with some amazing men through various love affairs, some difficult and some enchanting, but each time one ended I wondered if love would ever truly find me. It seems that no matter how bruised and banged up this little heart of mine gets, she keeps loving and loving and loving, as if forever channeling the *The Little Engine That Could*. My heart is always willing and available to expand just a bit more easily the next time around because she knows it is her true purpose here in this sacred flesh temple of mine. She knows this even though my rational human mind has closed her off and shut her down when the pain of loss felt too great to hold. Even in these moments, my precious guide continues to whisper and gently nudge my stubborn ass to see the broken bits as beautiful and necessary to my path of becoming the woman I was always meant to be. In the naiveté of my early twenties, I shielded and protected her from all sorts of heartache, while simultaneously allowing her to blossom into the multi-petaled lotus of my soul once I set her free again. I now recognize that my greatest strength and power as a woman lives in my heart's ability to strengthen and grow after each heartache. That is how this handsome and charming stranger found me on a balmy fall evening in an intimate nook of my favorite sushi restaurant.

We obviously matched and I felt my heart skip a beat as a smile swept over my rosy cheeks. I sent a sassy little message and waited with bated breath for the pilot with the dreamy eyes to respond. He was smooth, oh so smooth — with his words and with the way he made me feel somewhere deep inside. We had been here before — not in this lifetime, not in this way, but I knew him. I knew him in ways that are too hard to put into words, ways that make sense far beyond thinking and the logical mind. I just knew I had to meet this man. I needed to stand in his presence, feel his energy, anticipate his touch, swim in the depths with him, even if for just a moment. We set a date for the next evening to meet at Nishiki, a delicious sushi restaurant in my old Midtown stomping grounds, where the fish is fresh and the sake bombs flow freely. Truthfully, I almost cancelled the next day. I just wasn't sure this is how I wanted to date again, but the other ways I was doing it weren't turning up my Prince Charming either, so I showered, primped, and anticipated. It's a good thing I identify uncertainty, growth, and connection as my highest values because that's what stopped me from texting, "How about next time you're in town?"

I arrived first, and the waitress took me to a little booth in the back of the restaurant where I waited, a little nervous to meet this man to whom I felt an odd connection despite only exchanging a handful of words over text. It was perfect because I didn't have any preconceived ideas about who he was or what would happen. I had only excitement about meeting a beautiful new friend. When he showed up, I was immediately excited and yet somehow completely calm. We shook hands briefly, then shrugged and gave each other a half-hug, and then settled in quickly. He asked all the right questions, putting me at ease while waiting expectantly for my answers, looking deeply at me with those dark, smoldering eyes like he'd known me for eons from somewhere far beyond this time and space. I actually texted my roommate and BFF, "I'm in trouble with this one." It was a feeling I couldn't shake that foreshadowed the truth of my experience with him.

He told me stories of his life now and what it was like growing up in Africa and moving to the United States with dreams of taking to the skies someday. He shared with me the delights of fatherhood and travel and how it was navigating life as an Arab man living, learning, and studying airplanes in the United States after 9/11. We talked for hours about everything, from the ways in which we hide our deepest truths in relationships, to the meaning of his tattoos, to our relationships with our families, to how awkward dates with the wrong people can be. He told me I sparkle. I told him he makes me nervous. The last two were not vocalized until later, but in that moment, they were said through our energy when, inevitably, we touched intentionally for the first time.

He reached his hands across the table and took mine in his and asked, "Do you feel that? Do you feel that energy of our connection?" He then made a complete circuit, touching both my ankles with his instep while caressing my hands. We dove deep into each other through our extended, almost uncomfortable, unflinching gaze. Up until that moment, no one had touched my soul that deeply or intimately. As a student of Neo-Tantra, this was saying something. For those of you who may not be familiar, tantrikas are known for their eye-gazing and their desire to study and immerse themselves in the exploration of pleasure, intimacy, and connection. This felt simultaneously unnerving and primal, as raw and real as anything I'd ever experienced. Each moment with this enigma spanned lifetimes and yet it was gone in a flash. There was never enough time with him on the physical plane, that's for damn sure, but my soul knew every nook and cranny of his even after such a short time. Throughout the night, I settled even more fully into my watery, feminine core where this Scorpio goddess feels most alive and at home, a place never far off but not visited enough in previous years.

When he asked if the night was over, the part of me that knows better whispered, No matter whether you see him again or not, you will regret not spending these moments with him now. We planned to walk to the local dive bar to listen to music, enjoy the fresh air, and prolong the magic of the night, not knowing the path ahead and intrigued to know more. We started on our way down the block when he grabbed my hand again and said, "Wait." As he pulled me closer, placed his hand on my cheek, and looked deep into my soul yet again, I immediately felt an electric surge of anticipation. His lips touched mine and I swear time stopped. I had not been kissed like that before or since, and I can still feel the shadowy flow of the energy of that unforgettable moment as if it were yesterday. We held hands, skipped, and kissed our way to Old Tavern like giddy children who know they must be the very best of friends because it just feels so good, so right.

I witnessed myself at peace and aligned with my inner goddess in communion with a male presence that night because he held the container for me to embody my divine feminine essence. I learned what Goddess-worship by a fully embodied masculine man looks and feels like. It has stuck with me since that night and it has aided me well on my path; I've completely shifted my life upside down over the last year and a half as I explored the deepest recesses of my soul. The complex and enchanting Scorpio man played his guitar for me for the first time that night, and I haven't heard music the same since. To witness him playing life full-out, living his dreams, and embracing his magic was a sight to behold. It cannot be explained, only witnessed and felt. I believe that night we saw each other in a way that neither of us had experienced in this lifetime but which felt familiar because we had known each other in this way before. Over and over, we told each other how we'd not felt this way in a long while, or probably ever, while wanting the feeling to last forever secretly (or not so secretly, when you allow yourself to be seen so truly by another).

I met myself as the lover I'd never known myself to be — unabashedly free, completely available, vulnerable, and naked in every way. He strummed the strings of my body and heart as masterfully as he strummed the strings of that guitar. I can still feel the hot tracks of ecstasy he left upon my soul with each stroke and word he spoke to the part of me that knows only love.

In the following months, we navigated distance and the holy relationship in action. Wishing for another moment to feel his energy because of how I experienced myself in the fullness of my Shakti-Goddess nature, I pushed him and got triggered and witnessed the unhealed parts of myself show up. For those unfamiliar with the term "holy relationship," it refers to the opportunity for maximal growth and healing of our souls agreed upon somewhere out in the ethers where time and distance are not real (*A Course in Miracles* junkie here!). The holy relationship is the one that puts us face-to-face with all our demons. I got to know mine intimately, and there are no doubts that he met his. He got triggered and ran away twice. The beauty is that I didn't hold him back. I didn't cage the bird that my soul instantly recognized and that my body and mind instantly loved. Instead, I watched him fly. I watched him soar and I loved him more for being the man who taught me that I am a woman worth loving, especially because he couldn't love me in this lifetime. I now know unequivocally I am the woman so worth holding space for. I fell in love with him for all the ways he made me fall in love with me.

Through this sweet union, I realized that I never have to be afraid to love big and share it. I came to know that my growth and expansion occur with every new love, especially when that love is tested and I am challenged to question my beliefs and factor another's feelings into my reality. I matured and recognized that I am fully responsible for myself and my feelings, always.

Profound intimate relationships always bring up our baggage, if we let them. Long-distance relationships test our abilities to trust ourselves and another with our precious heart. I now stretch my wings and allow my tender, precious heart to fly with the freedom of knowing that whatever happens on this earth, only love is real. Love cannot be hampered, diminished, or discarded no matter how human we are, no matter how much we try to push it away or hide from it. Love always finds us. It embraces us and touches us in places we didn't know existed. It molds us and makes into the beloveds we were always seeking, the ones we forgot we were before life happened and things got complicated. The one that the eternal beloved within always reminds us to be.

I loved with my whole, open heart without regard to whether I might feel pain later on. I trusted myself to be my most courageous and trustworthy guide, listening to inner guidance; I was feeling what I was feeling in the moment and saying what needed to be said without care for the outcome. What I know is that this man came into my life to teach me that loving with abandon is my purpose here on earth. Sharing myself fully and authentically will never steer me wrong, no matter the circumstances that may come up. He taught me I still have a lot to learn and let go of in this lifetime. More than that, he showed me what it means to be naked and afraid but still determined to show up powerfully and gratefully in every moment. Wherever our paths may lead and wherever we may find ourselves, I know that I am a better woman because of his very existence. Thank you, darling man. Forever yours.

LOVE GIVES ME THE
POWER TO CHANGE
THE WORLD.

CHAPTER 18

Soul Connections

"Because love lasts."

By: Sara Gustafson

Sara Gustafson

www.sara-judith.com

ig: @sara_judith_stories | fb: @LightLoveWords

. . . .

SARA GUSTAFSON IS A writer, editor, dog mama, meditator, and spiritual seeker. She believes deeply in peace, social justice, and the Oxford comma. One of her single greatest joys in life comes from helping other people tell their story, and tell it well.

Sara lives with clinical depression and anxiety and is passionate about adding new techniques to her mental health management toolbox. These techniques include exercise, nutrition, meditation, prayer, journaling, and lots of naps and puppy snuggles. She speaks openly and honestly about her disease in order to help end the stigma surrounding mental illness and let others know they are not alone. The next step in Sara's career path will include becoming a mindfulness and meditation coach and leading meditation and writing retreats.

Born and raised in central Massachusetts, Sara has lived in seven U.S. states and overseas in South Korea. She currently lives in Japan with her husband and her fur-baby, Dex.

"IT'S TIME FOR EVERYONE TO SAY THEIR GOODBYES."

I did a double take at the nurse's words. Surely, she just meant that visiting hours were over and we needed to leave for the night, right?

I looked at my friends standing next to me and then down at Jeff. He was pale and still, far from the vibrant boy who'd given me my first kiss, who excelled at alternately pushing my buttons and making me laugh. The beeping of his monitors reverberated through my chest.

I clasped his hand and told him that we all loved him and would see him tomorrow. What I really wanted to say was that *I loved him*, but at sixteen (two days away from seventeen), I feared the power of those words. How vulnerable they made me.

The hour-long ride home from Boston Children's Hospital was largely silent. We were lost in our own thoughts, our own ways of processing. It was the summer before our senior year of high school; how did we find ourselves thinking about death instead of college applications and prom? While my best friend Kaithlyn, who's always been wise beyond her years, seemed to fully grasp what was coming, I remained naïve, or perhaps in denial. I believed we would make the drive back to Boston in the morning to rally at Jeff's bedside once again.

As I lay on Kaithlyn's couch that night, I was jolted from my half-drowsing state by the sense of a figure in the doorway. I couldn't make out any features in the darkness, just a hazy outline, but I somehow knew it was male. An unknown man appearing over me in the middle of the night should have sent me into a heart-racing panic, but all I felt was a sense of calm. The figure emanated peace, comfort. He seemed to be telling me that all was well. I waited for my eyes to adjust to the darkness, hoping to make him out more clearly, but he faded away.

The next morning we received a call telling us not to come to Boston. The decision had been made to remove Jeff from life support. Several hours later, he slipped away. My father held me as I took the call. It was the first time I ever saw him cry.

Jeff would have hated the way I handled his death. He spent our entire relationship (both our short-lived romance and our much stronger friendship) trying to get me to open up, to lighten up, to enjoy life, and not to take things so seriously. After his death, though, the fact is that I wallowed. I luxuriated in my grief like a pig in shit. I closed myself off, doors slamming shut around my heart like a fortress. I was terrified of loving again, of losing again.

Occasionally I thought of that hazy figure I saw in Kaithlyn's doorway. I thought of the comfort it gave me and the peace I felt. But for the most part, the lesson I walked away with was this: love cannot last. Ultimately, one way or another, it will go away, and all you'll be left with is pain.

When I fell in real, adult love for the first time and entered my first adult relationship a couple of years later, that fear came charging through my mind like a bull in a china shop. Self-sabotage became the name of my game, and I was damn good at it. Despite how deeply connected I felt to this man on every level imaginable, I looked for any excuse for why things shouldn't, wouldn't, couldn't possibly work out. My mother saw through me to what was actually happening. One night, nearly two years to the day that Jeff had passed, she called me out on my crap when I was venting my latest lame pretext (I was angry over the fact that my boyfriend insisted on buying me a birthday present even though I'd told him not to bother). I'd love to say her words changed me right then and there, but they didn't. The relationship ultimately ended because the sheer intensity of my feelings scared the bejesus out of me and so I cut and ran, multiple times.

My mother held my hands and stared deeply, unwaveringly into my eyes. "Sara, I will die before you. And when your time finally comes, I will be the first one down that big hill to wrap you in my arms. *Because love lasts.*"

How long I took to believe those words. And how very, very true they are.

The First Law of Thermodynamics tells us that energy can be neither created nor destroyed.[8] It simply changes forms. Love itself is energy. When we love someone, truly love them on a soul level, that love can never go away. It may shift forms throughout our lives, but it is always there.

I believe that we are here in this life to learn, to grow spiritually, and to help one another do the same. I've also come to believe that there are people in our lives with whom we've made agreements to do just that. Friends, family members, lovers, teachers, even strangers at the coffee shop — these soul agreements can show up in a plethora of ways. When two souls form such a connection, their bond persists in one way or another despite changes in the external relationship. This can be true even when we go through a traumatic break-up or when a friendship falls apart. Our loving feelings for that person may dissipate, and we might never see them again in this life, but it does not end our connection on a soul level.

Marianne Williamson writes:

> When we physically separate from someone we've been involved with, that doesn't mean the relationship is over. Relationships are eternal . . . Often, letting go of the old form of the relationship becomes a lesson in pure love much deeper than any that would have been learned had the couple stayed together.[9]

I feel that with my first love. Occasionally I'll hear a song or read a book that reminds me of him and I'll feel a loving warmth come over me. Not the old romantic passion, of course, but rather a spiritual love from my soul to his, an appreciation for the lessons I learned while we were together. It's as if our souls are waving hello.

It's a fact of life that relationships change and sometimes even expire. People die, romances end, friendships are outgrown. These changes are painful, but they also present us with some of our biggest opportunities for growth. In fact, that might even be the point of some of our relationships, their ultimate purpose. Some relationships may need to end in order for us to continue our spiritual and emotional development. We can only learn some lessons in times of upheaval. When a relationship ends or changes form, it may just mean that our soul agreement has been fulfilled, and we've done our job for each other.

Of course, as humans, none of us like change, especially when that change is painful. Many of us struggle to let go of relationships even when it is clear they have expired. Simply put, it's hard to say goodbye to someone we have loved. On some level, it's far more comfortable to cling to the past, to the familiar, than it is to grieve the relationship and walk into an unknown future. If we're unwilling to face the discomfort of truly letting someone go, we can find ourselves stuck in negative patterns for years — ruminating obsessively about the relationship; feeding feelings of anger or resentment or depression; numbing our feelings altogether with food, alcohol, drugs, work, or any number of other covers; or, in my case after Jeff's death, avoiding authentic relationships due to fear of further loss.

I've found the idea that our souls remain connected even after a relationship ends to be hugely comforting in times like this. Shifting my mindset from "I'm losing this person forever" to "I'm just saying goodbye to this person in their current form" allows me to let go a little more easily. I've also developed a ritual I use in my meditation practice when I face the need to let go of someone or something. It's my take on a cord-cutting meditation, made popular recently by Gabby Bernstein.[10] I call it my "Release to Rise Meditation."

Release to Rise Meditation

Important note: If you are struggling to release or process any kind of trauma, medita-tion and visualizations can sometimes act as a trigger. Please take any steps necessary to ensure that your environment feels safe for you before engaging in a meditation. I also highly recommend discussing any meditation practice with your mental health profes-sional or healer or with a trauma-informed meditation coach (which I fully disclose that I am not yet).

Find a comfortable posture in which you can relax while remaining alert. For me, this is a seated position on my meditation cushion (meditating while lying down means an instant nap for me).

Close your eyes (while some meditators prefer to gaze softly at the floor, this meditation involves visualization so is best done with the eyes shut).

Take a few deep yogic breaths, inhaling to the count of four, holding for the count of four at the top of the inhale, and exhaling to the count of four. Do this as many times as you need to slow your nervous system and feel present.

Call to mind the person you are struggling to release. Visualize them standing in front of you. This in itself might bring up some powerful emotions; allow those to come up. Continue breathing deeply as you give yourself full permission to feel whatever you are feeling. Know that if you get overwhelmed, you can stop this meditation at any time. If you need, internally repeat the words "I am safe here" as you inhale and "I am fully supported" as you exhale.

Imagine a beam of golden light expanding out of your heart and extending toward this person. With each breath, the light becomes stronger and stronger, dissolving any negative emotions associated with the relationship and leaving only love.

As you breathe, acknowledge the person's role in your life as a soul connec-tion and thank them for playing that role. Then tell them that you release them from your earthly relationship and that you give both of your souls permission to continue your separate growth. You might say something like, "Dear X, I know that we met in this life for a reason. I know that our souls agreed to engage with and learn from one another, and I honor that soul agreement. I thank you deeply for the lessons I learned in our time together. I now lovingly release our relation-ship as it was and welcome whatever comes next. We are now fully free to grow and develop as we are meant to, until our souls meet again."

Visualize the golden light enveloping the person. They smile and give your soul a wave as the light dissolves them, slowly and peacefully.

Take a few more moments to breathe in the feeling of release and love. When you are ready, gently wiggle your fingers and toes, stretch your neck from side to side, or make any other gentle movements to bring you back into the room.

I've found this ritual to be highly effective in reducing my tendency to cling to relationships and in deepening my appreciation of my soul connections.

I took years to fully embrace my mother's lesson, the idea that love lasts even beyond death. But once I opened myself up to the idea that Jeff and our love for one another had not just vanished into thin air, I started to feel him everywhere. I'd walk into a store and hear one of his favorite songs, one I hadn't heard since I was seventeen. I would dream about him and wake to feel the room filled with his presence.

One day, I went to get a pedicure. The woman in the next chair turned to me and said, "I know this will sound crazy, but have you lost someone close to you, a young man?" When I confirmed that that was the case, she continued. "I don't know if you believe in this kind of thing at all, but I'm a medium. I see him standing behind your right shoulder, poking you and laughing. He says he does that a lot." Since that day, sometimes when I'm deep in meditation, I'll feel a twitch in my right shoulder. I smile, knowing it's a hello.

I happened to be home in Massachusetts on the fifteenth anniversary of Jeff's passing. It had been more than a decade since I'd visited his grave, but I knew in my gut that I could find it again. As I drove around the cemetery, looking for just the right tree, just the correct right turn, a string of old songs from high school came on the radio. His way of ensuring that I would mark the day not with sadness but, as he always insisted, with laughter and with love.

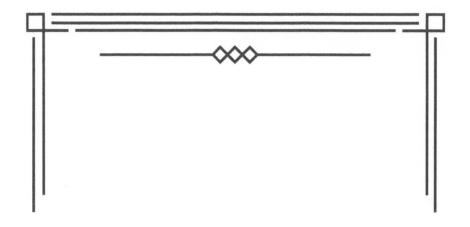

MAY I BE HAPPY. MAY I
BE HEALTHY. MAY I BE AT
PEACE AND LIVE IN EASE.

EPILOGUE

BY: SARA GUSTAFSON

The Sufi poet Rumi writes, *"The paths are many, but the goal is one."*[11] With love, the only way we can fail is if we do not open our hearts in the first place. The women in this book have opened their hearts in so many different ways — to themselves, to children, to parents, to lovers. They've also taken a massive, scary step in opening their hearts to all of you. It takes great courage to share personal stories so publicly, knowing they can be read, interpreted, and opined on by anyone. It's been one of the greatest honors of my life to lead this group of authors, and I feel such a deep love for every one of them.

I'm also deeply inspired by how each of these authors has worked to put love into practice in her life. Love truly is an action word and as I wrote in the introduction of this book, it is not for the weak. Living with an open heart is one of the hardest, if not *the* hardest, things we can ever learn to do. It requires us to look at the world's ugliness, to commit every day to see through it to the soulful core of things, and to work to make that core manifest in our lives. Author and social activist bell hooks refers to this work as living from a love ethic:

> A love ethic presupposes that everyone has the right to be free, to live fully and well . . . Commitment to a love ethic transforms our lives by offering us a different set of values to live by. In large and small ways, we make choices based on a belief that honesty, openness, and personal integrity need to be expressed in public and private decisions.[12]

Sounds a little daunting, right? But like all journeys, it starts with one small step. Reading the stories in this book has made me more mindful of the small steps I can take daily to live from a place of love, and I hope your journey with this book inspired you similarly.

There are countless actions we can take to bring a little more love into our world. Spend some time each day with yourself in meditation or prayer or whatever else connects you to your spirit. Eat more fruits and veggies, drink more water, and move your body in ways that make you feel alive. Slow down your morning hustle and take time to hug your family and tell them you love them. Perform random acts of kindness. One of my favorites is Friend-Care Friday, instituted by author and anti-racism educator Rachel Cargle, on which you send five dollars to a friend just to thank them for being them.

Set strong, loving boundaries. Practice listening without judgment, respond-
ing instead of reacting. Volunteer or donate to causes that are important to you.
Speak up against injustice and hate. Vote. Write a love letter to yourself or someone else, and send it. Offer to cook or clean for a friend who's feeling down. Play
with that crying toddler on the plane so Mom and Dad can get a break. Educate
yourself about issues in your community and how you can help. Plaster your bathroom mirror in love notes.

Whatever you feel called to do, know that your small loving act will create a
ripple effect through your family, your community, and your world. I see this book
as a collection of such acts: a handful of pebbles thrown into a vast lake by a family
of love warriors. I can't wait to see where these ripples go, and I hope you join us
on the shore.

Acknowledgments

For my mama. Thank you for the endless patience, love, and support. I know wherever you are, you are shining so bright. This chapter is for you, for me, for us. I hope you're proud.

\- Christine Esovoloff

Thanks to all my family and friends for believing in me until I could believe in myself. Thanks to Noelle and John for holding up the mirror and to editor Sara Gustafson for holding my hand.

\- Pam Davis

I would like to express my gratitude for my mother, Susan Norkett, who kept me afloat during hard times and always pushed me forward. I would not be where I am today, and I would not have been able to write this piece, without her.

\- Apryl Norkett

I want to thank my Mom for making me tough and kind. I also thank the students at Holy Family School in South Pasadena California, who inspired and encouraged me to write a chapter about how important it is to introduce to teenagers and adolescents to the simple practices of self-love.

\- Roberta Fernandez

To my mom for standing by me and being just what I needed while grieving your own loss. I know what love is because of you, and everything I am, you helped me to be. To my husband for never leaving. Thank you. For better or for worse, in sickness and in health. We made it. I love you.

\- Jess Harvey

*To Dave, Max, and Cinco. I love each of you to the moon and back
and am forever grateful for your love, humor, and mischief-making.
To my Mom, Heidi. Thank you for your support and confidence in
me as a writer. I can still hear you saying, "You're a great writer!"
even when I wasn't writing a word. And to Aunt Sue. I have so much
gratitude for you and for the way you modeled what it means to
have a "big heart" so very well.*

- Jess Reidell

*You've given me patience I never knew I had and filled my heart
with an abundance of love and admiration. I am who I am because
of all I've learned from you. You have shown me the importance of
hard work and determination and most importantly the necessity for
love — without it, none of this would be possible. Thank you, Dad,
for all you've taught me — then and now. I am my father's daughter,
I always was and always will be.*

- Maryann Perri

*To my loving and supportive parents who cheer me on and help me
persevere in all my endeavors. To Danielle, Austin, and Rio, who
lift me up with laughter and continue to teach me how to love. To
my amazing, gentle, and nurturing husband who believes in me, at
times more than I believe in myself. I am the lucky one who gets to
share my life with each of you.*

- Tamara Simpers

*To all the women who shared their hearts through words since time
immemorial. To my mama, who taught me to love with openness
and clarity. To those who supported me on my journey and those
who didn't — I love and honor you for teaching me to love myself
and others more deeply and truly.*

- Mandy Valpey

To Jeff, my angel. Thank you for still making me laugh and lighten up. And to all the others I've loved and lost, thank you for the soul connection.

- Sara Gustafson

I dedicate this chapter to my two amazing boys, Ryu and Luca, who helped teach me that not only do they deserve the best version of mama but that in order to be able to give them that, I first have to recognize that I am worthy of loving myself, too.

- Habiba Jessica Zaman

I would like to pay tribute to my mother, who struggled for decades while living in oppression and abuse but did not give up. She instilled the courage within us to continue moving forward in life regardless of the circumstances. She lost so much in life but still stands strong like a true warrior. Love you, Mom.

- Saira Amjad

My chapter is dedicated first and foremost to my daughter Rhea. I wish you all the love in the world and hope that you feel it in your own heart first. I want to also thank my husband for supporting all of my endeavors and showing me unconditional love. Finally, to my parents and my sister and family, who have always been there for me and always encouraged me to do better.

- Corinne Walsh Stratton

Endnotes

[1] Estés, Clarissa Pinkola. (1996). *Women Who Run with the Wolves*. New York, NY: Ballantine Books.

[2] Curtis, Richard (Director). (2003). *Love, Actually* [Motion picture]. United Kingdom: Universal Pictures Home Entertainment.

[3] Dobosz, Ann Marie. (2016). *The Perfectionism Workbook for Teens: Activities to Help You Reduce Anxiety and Get Things Done*. Oakland, CA, USA: Instant Help.

[4] Knaus, William. (2016). *Overcoming Procrastination for Teens: A CBT Guide for College Bound*. Oakland, CA, USA: Instant Help.

[5] About MARC. (2019). Retrieved from https://www.uclahealth.org/marc/about-marc.

[6] Aphasia. (2019). Retrieved from www.asha.org.

[7] Apraxia. (2019). Retrieved from www.webmd.com.

[8] The Laws of Thermodynamics. (2018). Retrieved from https://courses.lumenlearning.com/boundless-chemistry/chapter/the-laws-of-thermodynamics/

[9] Williamson, Marianne. (1996). *A Return to Love: Reflections on a Course in Miracles*. New York, NY: HarperOne.

[10] Cut the Cord: Practice the Cord Cutting Meditation. (2016). Retrieved from https://gabbybernstein.com/cut-the-cord/

[11] Harvey, Andrew. (1999). *Teachings of Rumi*. Boulder, CO, USA: Shambhala Publications.

[12] hooks, bell. (2018). *All About Love*. New York, NY: William Morrow Paperbacks.